MW00932754

ONE EYE *ON THE* WORLD

ONE EYE ON THE WORLD

JOHN L. SHIELDS

ARCHWAY
PUBLISHING

Copyright © 2020 John L. Shields.

All rights reserved. No part of this book may be used or reproduced by
any means, graphic, electronic, or mechanical, including photocopying,
recording, taping or by any information storage retrieval system
without the written permission of the author except in the case of
brief quotations embodied in critical articles and reviews.

This book is a work of non-fiction. Unless otherwise noted, the author
and the publisher make no explicit guarantees as to the accuracy of
the information contained in this book and in some cases, names
of people and places have been altered to protect their privacy.

Archway Publishing books may be ordered
through booksellers or by contacting:

Archway Publishing
1663 Liberty Drive
Bloomington, IN 47403
www.archwaypublishing.com
1 (888) 242-5904

Because of the dynamic nature of the Internet, any web addresses or
links contained in this book may have changed since publication and
may no longer be valid. The views expressed in this work are solely those
of the author and do not necessarily reflect the views of the publisher,
and the publisher hereby disclaims any responsibility for them.

Any people depicted in stock imagery provided by Getty Images are
models, and such images are being used for illustrative purposes only.
Certain stock imagery © Getty Images.

ISBN: 978-1-4808-8702-2 (sc)
ISBN: 978-1-4808-8700-8 (hc)
ISBN: 978-1-4808-8701-5 (e)

Library of Congress Control Number: 2020904062

Print information available on the last page.

Archway Publishing rev. date: 3/26/2020

Contents

Foreword

While I have traveled to many countries during my 75 years, there is not one which comes even close to our blessed United States. It's always been a privilege to be a Texan, U.S. citizen, and member of the Shields family. Maybe not in that order.

This collection of stories may not interest some, but felt it was owed to my children—Kristina Renee Shields Estes, Philip Michael Shields, and Kathryn Thompson—so they may understand who I am and why. It really came to be when Kristina gave me a small—very small—book a few years ago with a lot of questions about my life. Well, never at a loss for words, my life would not fit into those small pages. This collection of stories through my life offer a bit of history, humor, sadness, and joy.

My views of the world have been through my one eye, having lost the right eye when one and a half years old. Thus the title, and a bit of humor. Humor has always been extremely important to me traveling through the years. Keeps my mind active, and thoughts away from those of an old fellow. Really, some in their 50's are old. Poor souls. My guiding light the past 50 years has been "Two Steps Ahead Always". "Oops" will be added when I kick the bucket.

This also chronicles some of the people who played such a pivotal role in my life, and then almost 50 years in the newspaper industry. Those years were the Glory Years for newspapers in this country. The world changes as years go by, and, sadly, so has the newspaper industry. My career covered some of the most interesting times and events in U.S. history. I had a front row seat as a reporter, editor, publisher and supervisor of groups of newspapers.

The past 49 years were spent with my wonderful and beautiful wife, the former Janice Davis from Napa, California. She was always there supporting me and raising our children when we moved, advancing my career. We "only" lived in seven states and 11 cities during our marriage. That doesn't include Arizona after retiring. God Bless her, she's amazing.

It's been an interesting, rewarding career and life. Hope readers enjoy this account of our journey.

JOHN L. SHIELDS

The World through One Eye

My, oh my, 75 winters, springs, summers and falls have passed me by. Thankfully, my body and mind are still performing. Or maybe they are performing at 75 per cent, one per cent for each year. It's also possible that retention has always been at 75 per cent. If that's the case, it's scary to think how great I might have been with that other 25 per cent. But, so goes it!

Through 73 and one-half of my 75 years, I've viewed the many wonders—and some disasters—of the world through one eye. Well, actually, I've always had two, but one was glass during my early years. Thank God the plastic eye came into my life when I was probably around nine. Could have been earlier—or later— but really don't know. My parents knew, but they're gone.

At least I no longer looked like a freak sometimes depicted in horror films. Least it didn't feel that was the case. Some people still believe it just looks like a lazy eye. Of course it does, the eye just sits in the socket, not attached to anything. Whatta' you expect? Afterall, the only real function it performs is to make me look sort of normal.

At least one friend (?) says calling my looks normal is a far stretch, not even considering the eye. What does he know, he's from New Jersey. Need I say more? Might have been much easier just to have worn a black patch. Some girls might have found that sexy. Imagine that, me considered sexy. Not! My imagination doesn't go that far.

No longer freakish until I got older, but that is just a part of the aging process. That's supposed to be funny! Oh please, always have a sense of humor. Humor is good for the soul. Unfortunately, many never have humor or common sense. To prove my point, just look at what Congress does. Or doesn't do. Makes me want to require they sit in a corner for doing such a lousy job most of the time. Okay, that's just wrong. All of the time. Who knew public welfare paid so well?

Knew I should have ditched journalism when it was still an honest profession and run for Congress, Senate or even President. With no regrets, but things might have been different with another 25 per cent brainpower. Then again, maybe not. Based on performance, politicians seem to sort of function with brainpower in the teens. Politician without a screw loose? My imagination doesn't go that far, either.

By my count, 13 presidents that I truly remember: Harry Truman, Dwight Eisenhower, John Kennedy, Lyndon Johnson, Richard Nixon, Gerald Ford, Jimmy Carter, Ronald Reagan, George H.W. Bush, William Clinton, George W. Bush, Barack Hussain Obama, and Donald Trump. Math's still good alright, that's 13. Is it Friday? If I had possessed that other 25 per cent of brainpower, I could have held my own with these fellows. Take that to the bank, and hope you can find a teller. Well, maybe not with the Great Communicator Ronald Reagan. Okay, maybe there are a few more, but none with more common sense and knowledge of the common man or common woman. Do we really have common women? Or, common men?

When I was Young

The year is 2018. Oops, now it's 2019 since I kept adding to the story. During my lifetime, transformation affecting everything in the life of Americans has been the most dramatic of anytime in history. World War I had come and gone when I came along in 1942, a year after the U.S. entered World War II. It was an amazing time as brave Americans signed up to fight to save the world. They did so but thousands of lives were lost in battle. They paid the ultimate price for freedom for the world then, and future generations. Many today don't understand or appreciate their sacrifice, including many in Washington. D.C. Shameful.

Other Americans remained at home but were vital to the war efforts in so many ways, including building airplanes, ships, weapons, and producing food. And, yes, developing the bombs dropped on Japan to end the war. People in the world need to backtrack and learn how these brave soldiers fought and died to preserve the freedoms we have today. Don't know, but doubt you will find much about this in most school history books today. Hope I'm wrong.

Instead, many inept politicians find a way to get elected by an uninformed public. They continually bicker without an agenda for their constituents. Many immediately concentrate on how to get re-elected in order to collect handsome salaries and future benefits. Most undeserved, and much greater than most Americans. Strange how many become instant millionaires, often right after they leave office. Some while still in office.

One of the most important things we can do as Americans is honor those who serve in all branches of the military. Being militarily prepared is paramount to our freedom, and freedom of the world. Unfortunately, some in all generations have no clue the importance of a strong military. The world depends on the U.S. for protection. Thanks to Donald Trump, other countries are now having to pony up more for their protection. Note to past presidents: it's about time. A strong U.S. military is important to world peace. Unfortunately, Russia and China are increasing their military arsenals as this is being written. Then there are the bad boys in Iran and North Korea.

After the war, the United States became a changing nation with more automobiles and new highways enabling people to travel farther, faster. Television became available to almost every American. President Truman gave the first televised address from the White House in 1947. Thus began the transformation of getting news and entertainment from newspapers and radio to the new mediums. Today the many forms of social media allow everyone to have instant contact and news throughout the world. That's not necessarily a good thing. Many lack the skills to process what they hear or read. Anyone can post or say anything. It doesn't have to be true. Sad commentary.

Newspapers Forget Their Mission

While today's social media reaches millions instantly, it's also had a dramatic, negative effect. Nothing guarantees accuracy of what's posted. This is—unfortunately—sometimes the only way many get their news. As a former reporter, editor and newspaper publisher, that is extremely disturbing. Also disturbing is the rampant liberal bias in newspapers, television and radio today.

Newspapers—the public watchdogs—are being closed as they lose subscribers and revenue. They have always served as a beacon for freedom. Losing newspapers is unfortunate for the country. While some are not closing, they just lack the quality journalism and dedication to readers of those produced in the past. What I consider The Golden Years. My career in the industry was 1959-2007. I like to believe readers had more respect for newspapers during most of those years. They looked forward to the newspaper hitting their doorstep.

During my almost 50-year newspaper career, opinions were strictly limited to the editorial pages. Simply, opinions were banned in regular news pages. Then, some newspapers began labeling stories as analysis. That was not permitted where I worked and supervised newspapers in several states. Opinion belongs on the editorial pages, not in news stories.

For many newspapers, unbiased reporting is a thing of the past. It's even more true for television. The major networks are blatantly guilty of this sin. It's shameful, wrong, and dangerous. Many have lost the respect enjoyed in the past, and that saddens those of us who enjoyed those days. Now, the cherished first amendment is under threat by some. The world can only hope those who use its protection truly understand the significance for its inclusion by our forefathers. And, appreciate and defend it.

Many newspapers have lost their way. They have forgotten their mission and what made them successful. Community newspapers have always been the bedrock for providing local news to citizens. Unfortunately, hundreds of community newspapers have been purchased by companies focused on the almighty dollar. They squeeze and squeeze until there are reduced pages, fewer reporters and editors. Width of a page has been cut dramatically over the years. That means less space for news. Much less. That was partly driven by higher newsprint cost, and to maintain or increase profit. Most won't remember these changes impacting coverage. It has—bigtime.

Those are reasons why the number of U.S. daily newspapers has gone from over 1,700 in the 1950s to around 1,300 today.

After they have taken every last dollar, corporations have closed some and drastically cut pages and staffing in newspapers throughout the country. Staffing cuts are probably approaching 50% since the early 2000s. This will prove to be a tragedy for this nation. Understand, it is acceptable to maximize profit. Newspapers, like any business, must remain profitable. Because of the business climate, a number of newspapers throughout the country have also done away with their press. More local jobs gone forever. Less coverage gone forever. More bias, seemingly here to stay.

In today's technologically-advanced world, pages are easily designed, then shipped to another location for printing. Production of the newspaper has dramatically changed. It's now a computer world. I was there when reporters changed from writing stories on a typewriter to a computer. Noise of stories being banged out on the old manual typewriters produced a sweet sound in the newsroom. "Common" pages today are produced by some newspaper companies at a single location, and sent to distant locations for readers in their other newspapers. This "homogenized" news contributes to failure of the daily newspaper.

With reduced staffing and less onsite equipment required, some newspapers formerly in large buildings have now moved to a typical and much smaller office setting. This certainly would not have the same feel for those folks who worked in newspapers of the past. A dramatic change. Watching a press crank out thousands of papers an hour is very impressive. Smell of ink is a nice memory for many today.

Just prior to this book being submitted to publishers, the largest merger of newspapers in this country was announced by Gannett Company and Gatehouse Media. Gatehouse is the operating subsidiary of the New Media Investment Group, according to a news story. The purchase means 260 daily newspapers and probably over 400 other community newspapers will be owned by this group. It could also mean cutting employees and combining of operations for cost-cutting measures. This is often how payment of the purchase price is accomplished, sometimes by an investment group. Selling off the properties, and combining operations is often the method used.

This will not mean good news for dedicated readers of their news products. The industry has already been in a cost-cutting mode for years, trying to compete with a digital world. Time will tell, but I don't get a warm and fuzzy feeling for the hundreds of markets served by combining of so many daily newspapers in some of the country's best and major markets. Hope I'm wrong, but it may be just another nail in the coffin for the newspaper industry.

Newspapers have been essential for preserving freedoms enjoyed by Americans. They have been the voice for the common people.

The internet changed everything, and many publishers have not adapted. Publishers have forgotten that their main focus should be local news. Dramatic subscriber losses seem to be the norm in recent years. Online subscribers are often counted in daily subscriber numbers. That is just not the same as having a newspapers delivered to your driveway everyday. But, understand, number of subscribers is one of the criteria for advertising rates.

A newspaper's primary goal today should STILL be local news. If they remember this, they may not make as much money as before, but they can still be successful. Good, old-fashioned reporting in newspapers is needed to inform Americans. And, to hold government and public institutions accountable. Newspapers have been critical in keeping government honest. Sometimes, even that's not enough. Corruption is often rampant. Even—or perhaps particularly—in small and medium-sized towns and cities.

Publishers tend to forget their market includes parents, brothers, sisters, relatives, and grandparents. Those folks still want to read about their children, town councils, and other events taking place in the community. And, don't forget sports, obituaries and weddings. Those provide readership and success. Subscribers bring advertisers—and dollars. Those who may be directing newspapers from a corporate office must remember this if they wish to remain relevant and profitable.

While they also have an online presence, there is nothing like photos and stories from schools and other activities. However, an online presence for newspapers is helpful, and necessary in today's world. It's necessary in order to attract young—and old—readers, and to combat all the free sites for classified advertising. In the past, classified advertising provided an important portion of a newspaper's revenue. Online sites have dramatically impacted that newspaper revenue. Without a proper focus on the interest of subscribers, revenue from that source has also affected newspapers.

There are still many fine newspapers in this country with some very dedicated people. Hopefully, they will continue to fulfill their important mission. And, continue being responsible while remembering and appreciating the protection offered by the Constitution. It should not be abused.

Newspapers date back to the 1600s in this country. They have fought many battles through the years to maintain freedom of the press. It is essential to fight for this freedom even today. It would just be nice if those in the "media" today would recognize this, and just present the unvarnished news. Keep opinion where it belongs, and not offer opinion as a news story rather than a last minute sound bite.

A Changing World

While growing up, we often said that Ford (the car) meant FIX OR REPAIR DAILY. The auto industry was always interesting but it began changing in the 1950s. Better bodies, better motors, and more options were added. Then through the years, automobiles have become more dependable. That's a good thing for owners because today—with the proper care—automobiles can go hundreds of thousands of miles.

Many car buffs get excited when they see cars from the '50s and '60s with the beautiful designs. Today it is difficult to distinguish some automobiles from their competition. My first home ($26,000) was not even half of what some new cars and trucks cost today. Just not the same.

Another major change during my lifetime has been in the airline industry. Today, it's nothing to hop an airplane and fly across country or across the world. It was flying in comfort until they began squeezing more seats on every plane. For old people with rickety legs and knees, it is becoming a burden. Shame on those profit-squeezing companies. And, don't forget that stupid rule allowing all sorts of animal, including small horses, on the scrunched seating. Unbelievable!

Development of the modern airplanes is one of the true marvels during my life. I still find them amazing, and relatively safe. Especially compared to the automobile with inattentive drivers talking on cell phones and texting. Of course there are laws against such. But, they are ignored by many. Honk, honk, the light just changed. Move it.

The highways and streets are a marvel, although many are suffering from lack of attention. Those of my age appreciate the modern highway systems. We remember two lane roads. Now we zip around cities like Phoenix which has done a nice job with its highway system, accommodating a growing population.

The 1960s were often turbulent, but were some of the most interesting and most important years. I was in a class at West Texas College when an announcement was made that President Kennedy was shot in Dallas in 1963. It was a sad day for Americans. Famed broadcaster Walter Cronkite showed rare emotion when making the announcement that the first Catholic elected president was shot. Texas Governor John Connelly was also hit by rifle bullets from Lee Harvey Oswald, but survived.

No trial was necessary as shooter Oswald was then shot by Dallas nightclub owner Jack Ruby as he was led in handcuffs by police. Vice President Lyndon B. Johnson was quickly sworn in, and returned to Washington as president.

Unrest followed in Los Angeles during 1965 with rioting in the Watts section. More than 30 people died during those riots. It was a sign of the times, and changes to come in this country.

More shooting violence followed in later years as Robert Kennedy was killed during his 1968 presidential bid. Sirhan Sirhan shot him as he was walking through a hotel kitchen after making a speech in Los Angeles.

Great Civil Rights leader Martin Luther King was also shot and killed in 1968 while standing on a balcony of a Memphis motel. Those were some terrible years for this nation. They were years which saw dramatic, permanent change for this country.

It should also be mentioned that President Kennedy said the U.S. would land a man on the moon during the century. That historic event occurred July 24, 1969 when Neil Armstrong became the first man to set foot on the moon. Simply, it was an amazing feat and was a highlight for the 1960s.

War's Dramatic Impact

There were the Vietnam War protests, and growing demonstrations against U.S. involvement. The war dramatically escalated during those years. Lyndon Johnson won a four-year term after President Kennedy was killed. With so many protesting U.S. Vietnam involvement, Johnson did not pursue a second term in 1968.

After Robert Kennedy's 1968 murder, Hubert Humphrey won the Democratic nomination but lost to Richard Nixon, who had narrowly lost to JFK in 1960. Nixon later won a second term, but Watergate proved a fatal blow, and he had to resign. Vice President Spiro Agnew had resigned about a year earlier after being charged with political corruption. After resigning in disgrace, he pled guilty to income tax evasion. The federal corruption charge was dropped.

Vice President Gerald Ford, who had been appointed following Spiro Agnew, became president after Nixon's famous 1973 Watergate resignation. Those were sad times in American history. Nixon's resignation showed no one is above the law.

The 1968 Democratic Convention brought other protests and violence. Tom Hayden had become an activist in the early 1960s and was one of the protest leaders charged at the Chicago Democratic Convention. Others were also charged. The charges were later dropped. They were well-known during that era.

Hayden later cut his hair, was elected to the California Assembly, and the California Senate. He lost races for U.S. Senate and governor. Hayden showed it was possible to turn a corner after some interesting protest years.

The anti-Vietnam war activist had visited North Vietnam during the war and was allowed to return three American prisoners. The North Vietnamese permitted that gesture because Hayden had protested the Vietnam War. He later married actress Jane Fonda whose photo was snapped on a tank while visiting North Vietnam during the war. She will never live down the moniker "Hanoi Jane." She's daughter of acting great Henry Fonda.

Actor Ronald Reagan also made his appearance and was elected to two terms as California governor. He finally made it to the White House by whipping Georgia peanut farmer Jimmy Carter. Carter, a one-term president, was/is a fine gentleman. But, he failed badly as president. He's done some really good things after leaving the White House, including building homes for the poor. Should have given him a hammer and saw sooner.

Reagan was elected President in 1980, and reelected in 1984. He will go down as one of our greatest presidents. He brought this country back from the doldrum years of Carter, who should have continued as Georgia governor. Or, he could have continued to raise peanuts.

Oh, yes, President Reagan had a great sense of humor, and was known for handwriting many of his own speeches. He was a personable man, but was tough when needed. He told Russia, "Tear down that wall." Sure enough, the Berlin wall came down. It was a monumental time in history.

Those years were life-changing for this country, and set the stage for the future. While turbulent and violent years, it was interesting as a reporter and editor to have a front-row seat to history in California, a state leading the charge for change. Now, it's a sanctuary state with millions of illegal immigrants. They have been given voting rights in some elections. That's ridiculous. Some estimates have those here illegally around 20 million. Likely more with many flooding the border every month. Immigration laws should be enforced. The lackluster, do-nothing Congress needs to address this matter. They talk a lot.

Reagan's vice president, George H. W. Bush, followed him as president but got caught with his promise of no new taxes. Oops, that didn't work out so well and Bill Clinton then won two terms in the White House. Clinton weathered Impeachment proceedings, and the Monica Lewinsky scandal. He was a scoundrel in many ways. We just have to understand he was married to Hillary. Her true colors came out during her years as Secretary of State under Barack Obama, who was mostly a failure. Okay, so he was an effective speaker, but that did not translate into a successful leader of the world's leading nation.

Remember Obama bowing to some foreign leaders? It was sickening. Donald Trump is reestablishing the U.S. as the world's leader. While not the most eloquent of speakers he's chosen a different way of communicating with Americans. And, yes, he should sometimes temper his remarks, but he has been open to Americans, and makes himself available to the press. He's not perfect and makes mistakes like all presidents. But, he truly cares for our country. Not like those who continue tearing it down.

Back to My Story and Fond Memories

Now, back to my story. Yep, we lived on a cotton farm in a place called Swearingen, Texas, just outside of Wellington, when I was just one and a half years old. As the story was told to me in later years, a bully named Butch swung a harness hame (yes, that's correct) at my older brother, Billy. Oops! Butch, around 11 at the time, missed my brother but hit me square in my right eye. Just so you know, a harness hame is used for plow or draft horses. No tractor on our farm at that time.

For years I wanted to bust Bully Butch across the knees with a baseball bat, but got over that. Might even shake his hand today and thank him. Having only one eye helped make me the person I've been during my lifetime. However, being outspoken doesn't always make me popular with everyone, but that's okay. No one ever accused me of being a Caspar Milquetoast. If you don't know that name, visit Webster's. Only so much room for my stories.

After being hit by Butch, off to Amarillo—about 100 miles north—we went. A sweet man named Dr. Streit gave my parents the bad news and removed my eye. Later, I was fitted with a glass eye. Unfortunately, it was heavy, bulged and resulted in a lot of teasing—and fights—in my early years.

Must say, it made me tougher as a youngster. That and the long-handled underwear which showed through my shirt sleeves. Hey, we were poor and coats were in short supply. Needed to stay warm, and that was the purpose of long-handles. At least until years later when wearing them without a shirt became trendy with some who were mentally deficient. Still are to this day. That's supposed to be funny. So laugh, improve your day.

When older and no longer ashamed of having one eye, people would ask how I lost my eye. "I got in a fight when I was one and a half, but you should have seen the other guy." It takes a few seconds, then they get the joke. Ha, ha! Never said people I've met are at the very top of the I.Q. chart. However, most are among those with common sense and carry on normal conversations. Well, maybe my morning coffee acquaintances and our discussions would not be considered normal. After all, two are from New Jersey.

Our next farm home was an old house and we could actually see a few cracks in the wall, wind coming through during the cold winter. To keep warm, I sometimes slept between my two older sisters in a feather bed. Mother would heat bricks, wrap them in a towel, and place them at the bottom of my feet. The only heat was from a coal stove in another room, or the wood kitchen stove.

Well, wouldn't you know it, we got electricity about the time I was four, but it provided no heat. At least we could listen to an old radio. Maybe get a couple stations. When I was around six, we moved to a city. Guess 25,000 collective souls qualifies as a city.

Should also mention that we had an Ice Box on the farm. It's just what the name implies. My dad would get large blocks of ice and place in the Ice Box to preserve food. The cistern was also used to keep the cow's milk cold. The apostrophe in cow is correct since we only had one. Just try imagining having to use an Ice Box today. No refrigerator, no freezer, microwave—or electricity. Perish that thought. How far we've come. How spoiled we've become with all our electronic gadgets. People who lived before these appreciate many of the modern conveniences available today. But, some we could do without.

Just give me my smoker where I can do some of the finest pork ribs west of Texas. Little honey and beer give the sauce a sweet flavor, and lemon pepper adds a little tartness. Remainder of recipe is a secret. May want to market John's Barbecue sauce someday. Should I outlive my retirement funds, I will need that money.

While recalling many fond memories, a favorite was Daddy taking the family to pick cotton for other farmers. He gave this little tyke (me) a bag about a third or half as large as a regular 8-9 foot sack. Down the cotton rows I went picking bolls. Now that was a real family outing. To make money. Nice family outing on a hot day.

My sister Helen, now 88, would pack 100 pounds of cotton in that long sack. She tells me that Daddy would tell her not to fill it totally full, that someday she would pay for dragging that much weight. But, we were paid by the pound. Maybe that's why she experiences back problems today. Daddy knew best, but we did not always listen. The Shields were known to have a stubborn streak.

Our family never shied away from hard work. While not necessary, Helen—until recently—worked 15-20 hours a week at a gas station-pharmacy-restaurant-gift shop in Clarendon, on the main highway from Amarillo to Wichita Falls. Kept her active, and the owners and their children have been considered family for many years. But, two recent falls made it necessary to quit working. That's unfortunate since she enjoyed being out of the home and meeting people.

Picking cotton was also when I first became acquainted with one of my lifetime staples—Van Camp pork and beans. It was one of the foods we could take to the fields without spoiling. Still love them today. And, no, don't try to give me those Campbell's pork and beans. Yuk! Pork and beans also help the body perform a natural function. While a bit in dispute, Van Camp pork and beans had their origin around 1880, so they've been popular for many years. Plenty time to reach perfection. Unfortunately, they recently changed the label, making them difficult to locate in my local Walmart. Think that would have made Sam Walton unhappy. Don't recognize the name? He started Walmart down in Arkansas.

A favorite memory as a youngster was stopping at a service station outside of Wellington, on the highway to Shamrock. That was close to the turnoff to our farm after the move from Swearingen. Sometimes, Dad had enough money to treat us to a cold soda from the outside Coca-Cola tub. It was loaded with water and ice to keep sodas cold. That water and ice were very cold, even on a hot day.

My favorite drink was either a Nehi strawberry or orange soda. Some will remember the orange then came in a dark brown bottle. That was a real treat for a farm kid. My oldest sister, Helen, remembers bringing a friend home, and she enjoyed canned peas. Stopping at the station, my dad had enough money to purchase a can of peas for the girl. God Bless my Dad, he was a charitable, caring soul.

As I said earlier, my folks—Buster Cecil and Laura Modene (Mitchell)—moved us about 100 miles northeast to an oil boom town called Borger, Texas. Farming was not supporting the family of five kids. Helen got married before the move. She was only a semester away from graduating high school in Quail, but marriage to the love of her life, C.E. Welch, was calling.

Texas Rangers Tame Wild Town

Prior to my youth, Borger had been tamed and was a thriving city, unlike when oil was discovered in 1926. After black gold was found, the governor sent the Texas Rangers to town to deal with violence, prostitution, gambling and other crimes. Rangers were sent in 1927, and again in 1929.

During Borger's early years, it was described as a rather wild place. At one point, some 45,000 lived in the area for work. The city is named after Missourian Asa (Ace) Borger. Never one to miss an opportunity, he and a partner purchased property and sold lots. Within six months they reportedly had $1 million. Lot of money for the time.

Borger was later killed by the county treasurer. Charged with embezzlement, he was supposedly upset that Borger would not bail him out of jail. When the man did get out of jail, he caught Borger in the Post Office, shooting him five times with a pistol.

Arriving in Borger, we moved in with Papa (Joseph Lonnie) and Mama (Ida) Shields (Hickman), my grandparents, until my dad got a job at a lumber yard. He worked there until he was hired by Phillips 66. Phillips virtually owned the town, with several different plants around Phillips and Borger producing gas, rubber and carbon black.

(At this point I pull an Elizabeth Warren—remember her claim of being Native American?—and tell you my family has Cherokee and Choctaw blood. Looking at Papa and Mama Shields confirmed that for me. Papa always smoked those old Roi Tan cigars, and Mama kept a large Folger's can beside her chair for spitting out her snuff. Story is that a great-great-grandmother was an Indian medicine woman. Yep, seems I'm legit, and proud of it. Didn't know this until later, or I would have played the part of an Indian rather than a cowboy as a youngster. Could have used those rubber tipped, arrows rather than my cap-shooting pistol).

In the 40s, Papa was a deputy sheriff in Wellington, Collingsworth County, and later a policeman and constable in Borger. Not one to abide nonsense from the bad guys, he had some truly interesting stories from his law enforcement days. He was a tough hombre with a pearl handled .45, and a blackjack to get attention if necessary. Papa was my hero as a child.

The carbon black plant was the worst, blowing soot for miles, settling on clothes hanging on the lines outdoors. That carbon black not only covered Mother's wash, but settled on homes, cars, grass, sagebrush and mesquite trees in the pastures. The government, during its early regulatory growth period, eventually required filters. It took care of most of the soot, and cows in the pastures were no longer unnaturally black. Who would have known Hereford cattle were actually a different color than black?

We lived in a half of an old quonset (sort of), bolted together with 2x8 boards. In later years my Dad bought it and paid $9 a month, as I recall, to lease land for the house. He also added on after ripping out one side so it was then half of a quonset and half a normal house. But it was home. The street, such as it was, had no paving, just red dirt. Our street was named Mary. Why, I don't know. Don't care. Wouldn't have made a difference if it was named Harry, George, or Elizabeth. Maybe Mary had an entertainment venue in the early days of Borger. Or, maybe the land owner had a mother named Mary. My parents did later purchase another home after my departure where the street was paved. A proud day for them.

From my bedroom window, I could look across a little more than a mile and see the 24-hour flame used to burn off sour gas at the Phillips 66 Refinery. The company owned several hundred homes, and the town was called Phillips. Some very small shotgun houses were actually directly across the street from the refinery.

The town of Phillips had a hospital, high school, small downtown, and Sutphen's Barbecue, the best mesquite smoked ribs anywhere. When a teenager eating there with my family, a waitress rushed over and asked if anyone knew how to use a fire extinguisher. The smoking pit was ablaze. I took the fire extinguisher and quickly put out the fire. We ate free that night at their insistence. Glad we already had our ribs before the fire. Believe it later burned, and the restaurant relocated to Borger, about four miles away.

Sometime later, Phillips moved all the homes to secure their operations. For years it was possible to drive right through the plants, but it was a changing world making more security a necessity. Perhaps it was because of a rumor that the gasoline production could be a target for enemies in case of a war. There was also a road passing through Phillips to the Canadian River and Plemons Bridge. The bridge was used for Roman Candle fights (that was really stupid), and to toss back a beer or two in later teenage years.

Seems appropriate now to share a story about Frank Phillips the oilman. He had visited Borger sometime after oil was struck in the area. As the story was told to me, cars were not so fast during the 1920s and '30s. During a late 1920s fuel test on Highway 66, the car hit 66 miles an hour. That was when the 66 was added and the company became known as Phillips 66. Today the company is known as Conoco-Phillips.

A friend of mine since we were probably 6 or 7, took me to his dad's home one day and it was located across the street from the refinery. We went in and he opened the refrigerator. He pulled out a roll of bologna. We ate. It was my introduction to rolled bologna. Still love bologna today. A meat for kings, and also tastes good fried. Sort of like ham. There's a tip for those famous television chefs. Do you hear that Guy Fieri?

That, fried foods and bacon. Should mention that one of the delicacies at our home was biscuits with red-eye gravy made from sausage grease and a little water. It melted in your mouth, and plowed right through the arteries.

Quart of Grease a Week

At the Shields' household, if you weren't digesting a quart of grease a week, you weren't eating right. Might as well die happy with a full tummy, right? Probably good we didn't have routine six-month cholesterol testing in those days. Likely the chart wouldn't have gone high enough. Certain death would have been predicted in today's world. But, both my parents lived into their 80s. If I make that, it will be in spite of all the preservatives in today's foods. That, not the grease, may kill me.

While not rolling in cash—yeah, it's a cliché—we always had plenty to eat, although not always with meat. Sausage and bacon were staples. Couldn't have survived without the hogs. Until this day, some of my favorite foods are pinto beans, cornbread, and fried potatoes. My Mother was very creative when it came to cooking, especially with her 600 or so quarts of fruits and vegetables she would can each year. You could almost see through her beautiful wild plum jelly and pear preserves.

Not to mention how she would get dozens of ears of fresh corn, put them in a brown paper grocery store bag, and place them in a freezer. Can still taste the freshness today. Tasted like it just came from the cornstalk. The freezer did come along later in life. Before that, my dad might kill a hog or purchase part of a beef. That sometimes went in a locker where he paid to keep it frozen. Control yourself now, but when Daddy butchered a hog, we had pork brains scrambled with eggs. A great delicacy—and delicious. Yummy! If that thought bothers you, then just think about where your eggs come from. Perhaps you should become a vegetarian if that is too troublesome.

My parents were the greatest and no one came to our home during a meal without eating. Or at least having a biscuit and jelly. Those were the days when folks did not have to call ahead. Couldn't for years anyway because we had no phone. Since my Mother's biscuits were to die for, no one ever said no. She had a large wooden bowl. Ingredients were just tossed into that bowl, not measured, and the most amazing biscuits would soon be on the table.

Fresh cornbread cooked in an iron skillet came with every meal except breakfast. Mainly because it was quickly consumed. All my family worked hard, and Mother's great cooking served the same purpose as gas to an automobile. Thanks to the pinto beans we produced our own gas.

My folks were the most honest, common sense people I've ever known. Best parents ever. Out of necessity, my Dad learned to do carpentry, mechanics, and plumbing. There was nothing he wouldn't tackle because he didn't have money to pay for repairs on the house or car. A jack of all trades and a very sweet, totally honest man. But he also knew how to haggle when buying. No doubt that's where some of my negotiating skills originated. Served me well in my newspaper career negotiating with unions and major advertisers.

My dad also added barbering to his talents when my brother Jimmy and I were young. Yes, this saved money. Dad first bought the old hand clippers, and I can still remember my hair being pulled by those things. But, dad improved each time, and our haircuts were not bad. He got even better after he purchased some electric clippers.

Again, I must fill in here just a bit about the one eye. While not remembering the exact age, it must have been when around nine that my folks took me back to Dr. Streit in Amarillo. Somehow he managed to fit me with a plastic eye, new on the market. What a wonderful difference. Perfect fit, color was fantastic, and I became a new boy. After retiring to Arizona, had my good eye examined in Mesa. They informed me there was an optometrist on staff who also makes artificial eyes.

When he examined my plastic eye, he asked how long I had it. Told him around 60 years. He was amazed, and noted that was extremely unusual. Sometime through the years, the white of the eye had been enlarged because my head had grown. Yeah, I know, some people always accused me of having a big head.

Anyway, he made me a new eye, then a second because the first wasn't just right. So, today, a couple extras are in a drawer at my home in Queen Creek, Arizona. But, he thought my eye around for so many years was one of the best he'd ever seen. Thanks, doc, feel better already, and don't feel even a bit freakish. My friend (?) still disagrees. But remember, he's from New Jersey.

Just one more one eye story, please. While writing this, my new neighbor, a vertically challenged Italian, turned 70. Regardless, he's a fine fellow and we have become good friends. Maybe he won't feel the same with this story included. Anyway, his sweet, pretty and younger wife was throwing a surprise birthday party for him.

Well, explained to his wife that I just happened to have a couple extra eyes. Thought we might just have a little fun. After the meal the 16 people were just sitting, visiting. All of a sudden I whipped off my glasses and hollered "damn this hardly ever happens." With my right eyelid closed, I then held up one of my extra eyes. People gasped. Birthday boy, sitting across from me, said "bullshit."

Okay, end of suspense. Just showed them it was an extra eye. Most did not realize I have a plastic eye. Surprise and relief, followed by laughter. Mostly. Time to toast the birthday boy.

Tapping Plastic Eye Does the Trick

After going to Frank Phillips Junior College for two years in my hometown of Borger, then enrolled at West Texas State College in Canyon, Texas. (Yes, I'm getting ahead of my story, but it has to do with the one eye). Will get to this later, but suffice it to say that I was the sports editor at the Canyon News while at West Texas. While covering a basketball tournament in Lubbock, Texas, a sportswriter from the Abilene Reporter-News was next to me. The Reporter-News was a good-sized morning and afternoon daily.

The fellow sportswriter was named Mike Wester and he said they had an opening in sports. Well, I had just enrolled in the second semester at West Texas, and had lucked into being a reporter/sports writer. Earlier had thought becoming a teacher could be a career. That really did not tickle the cockels of my heart, so I became a sportswriter in Abilene. Hot damn, no more schooling. Just went with educating myself about the world by writing for newspapers. And, what an education. Learned more about the people, all levels of government, schools, and the world. And,it beat heck out of a classroom.

That was in early 1964 and Selective Service was still actively drafting those not attending school. Many today—as they did in the Vietnam War—would go ballistic if they received a draft notice. Then, it was either go to college, get a medical deferment, or go into the service. Or, as some did, move to Canada or some other place out of the United States. At that time they were considered draft dodgers. Years later they were forgiven.

Not long after arriving in Abilene to begin work, my notice from Selective Service arrived. It's important to note that I registered shortly after turning 18 as required. Their office was in the basement of the Borger Post Office. The woman informed me I could be subject to immediate draft, being a few weeks late in registering. She then asked about any disabilities, and informed her about my one eye.

The woman looked at me, obviously didn't believe me, and told me it was serious to lie. Emphasized again about my one good eye. Well, the right eye was good, too, just plastic. She apparently did not place that information in my paperwork. Didn't take long for that to become obvious.

Received my draft notice in Abilene, and reported to Selective Service. Again, explained to the Sergeant about my one eye. "Are you Communist?," he asked. Told him no, and I was here if they wanted me. Then tapped my plastic eye, and asked if he could do that. Never heard another word.

They obviously didn't want a fellow with a plastic eye in the Army and Vietnam. Although not serving in our armed forces, I have always supported and have tremendous respect for those who do. They keep us safe in a turbulent world. It's also a great and rewarding career for many, including two of my nephews. It's also a good time to salute the great World War II soldier Audie

Murphy, a Texan, and the most decorated soldier. That's for those who don't know history.

I'm still available if they want a 75-year-old. That's highly doubtful. Maybe I could just be a greeter at a Marine or Army base. Sort of like they do at Walmart. With my experience, should at least be a sergeant from the start. Lacking a college degree, would have no expectations of being an officer. But, could handle if they chose to do so.

Okay, just one more story about the one eye before proceeding. After accepting a job in South Lake Tahoe, California a couple years later, visited Motor Vehicles to get a new driver's license. The employee told me to remove my glasses and place my face to a machine to take the eye test.

The man asked how far I could see down the chart. Told him I did not see a chart. He made adjustments twice, but still could not see a chart. Then it occurred to me. "Are you only testing my right eye?" "Yes," he said. Problem solved. He tested my left eye and passed the test, no problem. Okay, enough of the one eye saga. Onward to other events in my exciting 75 years.

Through the Years

Got the one eye stories out of the way for now, so let's jump back to when I was about 6 and 7. Learned to hustle and make a little money by gathering scrap metal, bolts and copper. Soda and beer bottles also brought me some coin. Then graduated to selling Cloverine salve door-to-door. They sent me a 12-pack, I sent them money, and they would send me a prize. Cloverine was 25 cents per container, if memory serves me correctly. Salve was supposedly good for a lot of ailments.

My first sales experience certainly helped me later in life after becoming a daily newspaper publisher and calling on major accounts. Of course advertising contracts brought a great deal more money than the quarter for Cloverine salve. Principle was the same. Just pitch the product.

One of the most valuable lessons in life became obvious to me when either 10 or 11-years-old. At that time, you had to be 12 to be a carrier for my hometown newspaper, the Borger News-Herald. While not old enough, the importance of knowing someone in the right position has remained with me my entire life. As I recall, my Dad was in Odd Fellows with a wonderful gentleman named Sam Duke. Well, Mr. Duke just happened to be the Circulation Manager for the Borger News-Herald.

A route about a mile from my home came open, and I was given the route. Papa and Mama Shields lived on that route and the newspapers were dropped at their Bunton Street house Monday through Friday. I would sit on their living room floor. If the News-Herald was 12 pages or less, my fast little fingers could fold all 125 newspapers in about five minutes. If more than 12 pages, I would normally use rubber bands. If folded width-wise, a 14 or 16-pager could still be folded, just very bulky and it might pop loose when tossed to the porch. Into my two bags they went, carrying on my shoulders.

Yet today, I can still quickly fold newspapers, or a piece of paper using that method. At a restaurant, waitresses must wonder when they see a napkin folded in that manner. Likely they unfold the napkin looking for a message. Sorry, no message just an old habit. My memory is still working.

My friend (?} is amazed and still has me demonstrate when a new person shows at our morning coffee gatherings. Never received a newspaper folded that way in all my years. If newspapers continue to get smaller, I might be able to make some extra coin teaching that method. Save the rubber bands—and the environment. Might add that there would likely be complaints because it creates a few creases in the pages. It was accepted back in my youthful days. Not so much when people pay more than a nickel for a newspaper.

Often on Sunday mornings, my Dad would drive down the middle of the streets. I would sit on a fender, holding onto the hood ornament of his 1950 Ford and toss newspapers to both side of the streets. Sunday's Borger News-Herald was larger, and it was tough to ride my English racer bicycle with a full bag on each shoulder. Did I mention that all except one street on my route were dirt and rocks? Of course I took some tumbles, but my plastic eye always remained in the socket.

My sales techniques improved during the time as a newspaper carrier. It should also be mentioned that subscription price was 25 cents—you heard that right—a week. My cut was a nickel, plus any tips. The News-Herald, it seemed, had a subscription drive underway at all times. Carriers could win all sorts of prizes. In order to qualify, a carrier needed to sign up as many customers as possible. Only so many top finishers could win. New customers must agree to subscribe for at least six weeks for me to count in the contest.

Not everyone on my route subscribed, but I became very adept at convincing enough to sign up for six weeks in order to be a winner in the various contests. So, yes, my 125 subscribers would go up and down.

Fortunately, a cheap motel was located just behind the Star Lite Lounge on my route. Oil field workers would stay in the motel for months at time. And, how could they tell a one-eyed 10-year-old they couldn't afford $1.50 for six weeks delivery to help him win a contest? Some would then quit, but would subscribe again during the next subscription contest. Genius at work. Didn't make the six-week rule, just used it to win contest prizes.

One of my cherished prizes was a huge Webster's Dictionary. Somewhere, Mr. Webster disappeared years ago. For being a winner in other contests, I enjoyed trips to the horse races in Raton, N.M. and to an amusement park in Oklahoma. That was my first time ever to ride in bumper cars. Still have the News-Herald photo of winners in that contest. I was the smallest and youngest in the group. Competition got my salesman juices flowing at a young age. And, the coins still had silver. Wish I had kept some of those to sell when price of silver skyrocketed.

Winners in another contest were taken swimming by district managers. We had about four managers who would drop bundles of papers to carriers at their homes each day. Highlight of the swimming party was when they would toss silver dollars, 50 cent pieces, and quarters into the shallow end of the pool. Carriers would then dive to see how much money they could collect at the bottom of the pool. Not being a great swimmer, I was happy they tossed the silver coins in the shallow water. That was followed by hot dogs and soda. One of my favorite contests.

Years later as a publisher I won company contests for all-expense paid trips to the Cayman Islands and Hawaii. Losing is not in my wheelhouse.

It was while delivering the newspaper one of my most valuable life lessons was learned about honesty, and helping those in need. Many folks on my route were poor, but they wanted the newspaper. That and the radio were often their main connections to the outside world.

One customer in particular—an elderly lady—would get up to six weeks behind on her weekly quarter payment. When it would get a dollar or more in arrears, she would plead that she couldn't owe for that many weeks. Knowing she had little money, I would ask how much she believed she owed. We might settle for 75 cents or a dollar.

That lesson taught me a great deal about life and honesty. It was hard work for my nickel a week profit. Yet, I would settle for what she thought she owed, absorbing the loss. If someone would cheat a poor 10-year-old, then it was necessary to be aware of dishonesty in life. My generosity cost me then, but the lesson served me well throughout life. While it did not seem so at the time, it was a cheap lesson preparing me for the real world.

In short, not everyone is honest. That became very evident when talking about big dollars. There are no degrees of honesty. Either you're honest—or you're not. Doesn't mean you can't negotiate, however.

On a hot summer day, fortunately, there was a Dairy Queen located at the end of my newspaper route. That often meant a great foot-long chili dog or, maybe, a root beer float. Nothing tasted better, unless it was a cold mug of A&W root beer, but that was not on my route.

Early School Years

My parents, as noted, were the best but—like many of their time—dropped out of school early to work. As I recall, they completed the eighth grade. However, they were very devoted to the Baptist religion, and my Dad was an avid reader of The Bible. Like most households during those years, he read the daily newspaper. An intelligent, self-taught Dad. But, he always had Mother write the checks.

In Texas at that time, a child had to be 6-years-old by September in order to enter first grade. I did not attend kindergarten, and was almost seven before beginning first grade. But when I did start school, the first five years were the most important learning years of my education. There is no substitute for reading, writing and arithmetic as taught by my teachers. And, believe me, Mrs. Biever, Mrs. Carr and a few others drilled those home.

During my first few years, I would often take home two or three (short) books each day, read them and return them the following day. To this day I am a voracious reader. Trust me, teaching to read is one of the most important things a teacher can offer a student. And, they would have us read to the class. It was difficult watching some classmates struggle with the three subjects mentioned above, especially reading.

In those days, a few had to repeat a grade if they could not meet the minimum skills. Today some finish high school, maybe even college, without some of the basic skills. That's just wrong, and a black eye for some schools. Yeah, I know, here come the letters, but I'll check the spelling. That's not meant to discredit so many great, devoted teachers and educators. But, it could be a reflection on some school systems today.

Fond memories include spelldowns, and also putting two to four students at the chalkboard. Then, the teacher would read off numbers for adding, subtracting, or multiplication. In the early grades it might be single or double numbers. Later it might be a series of four numbers. When the last number was given, I would have already added all the numbers in the right column. Friend C.W. Howell was a tough competitor in those little math competitions. Believe he later became a principal or superintendent in southern Texas.

Reading books helped me become one of the better spellers in my classroom. We were also taught phonetics. Can a computer, calculator or hand held device teach these skills as well? Instinct tells me no. It's sad when making a purchase today, and giving three pennies in order to receive quarters or dollars in return, rather than more pennies. That confuses so many cash register clerks with few math skills. Really sad.

In junior high, my first hourly paying job was when I was 14. Darby's Restaurant was across the street from the Dairy Queen on my former newspaper route. Leland Darby had a large, beautiful house and a gray and white Cadillac right next door. Mr.

Darby hired me as a dishwasher at 40 cents an hour. To me that was bigtime, and $16 a week.

Let me tell you though, washing the big pots and pans was tough for a skinny kid. And, taking plates from the dishwasher's hot water left my hands very pink. Most laws do not allow employees of this age today. Not many would accept such a job today anyway. Got to be on a phone or constantly playing games on those many devices. Wash dishes? No way.

Mr. Darby's father-in-law, Mr. Sharpe, was the butcher. He taught some tricks of the trade, and how not to slice my fingers. Doubt any restaurant today would let a 14-year-old use those sharp butcher knives, or the meat slicer. Without a doubt, Darby's had the best chicken fried steak covered with white gravy EVER! And, I even got to do some of the cooking.

Thanks for the opportunity, even though it was a mile walking home at 11 p.m. It was an experience which benefitted me during life. Lessons well-learned. Learning and working hard became my mantra for success in life. Are you listening, Sean Hannity, even though I painted no houses like you?

Another memory was having the money to buy myself a red, snap button, western shirt with those wages. Also bought my younger brother Jimmy a yellow shirt to match to start school. And, boots and real Levis. Those came from Dolly's Western Store. By the way Dolly was a man, and there was no doubt.

Sweet, cherished memories.

Onward with Schooling—and Work

Entering sixth grade, I already had the important basics useful throughout life. Plus, I had a wonderful and, yes, one-eyed teacher named Mr. Snider. A big classmate (sort of fat) sucker-punched me in the good eye one day. That made Mr. Snider very upset. He administered the board of justice to my classmate, and never had another problem with fatty. Mr. Snider and I sort of saw eye-to- eye, you might say. Yep, that's a pun. He was a sweet man and a fine teacher.

In the eighth grade, a teacher who liked me gave me one of the most important gifts of life. She thought I was associating with the wrong crowd, and told me she was placing me in a typing class the second semester. When we talk about important moments, that was a game-changer, eventually leading to a wonderful life and successful newspaper career.

I took to the typewriter like ink on newsprint. Then opted to take typing class in 9th grade. Thought it would be an easy class. It's been years, but Larry Moore and I were possibly the only boys in with all those girls. Not too bad.

Enjoyed it so much, then took typing (no computers then) as a sophomore. Whipped along, maybe 75 words a minute, and that included taking off five words for each mistake. Were the girls jealous? Maybe. Okay, probably. My hands still fly over the computer keyboard after all these years. Stay away, arthritis. Stay away dementia. Stay away alzheimers. Leave this old fellow alone.

In the ninth grade, I was also washing dishes at the Cedar Lanes Bowling Alley cafeteria, and could save time by typing lessons. Used my wages to purchase a typewriter. It was also neater than my handwriting because I was always in a hurry, short of time. However, those big cafeteria pots and pans did not help the back, bending over deep sinks. But we ate free, and the pies were yummy.

One memory from that bowling alley makes me laugh yet today, but quit after the incident. The manager (believe he also managed the cafeteria) was chasing me one day when I was teasing him about something. He was a big man, and I was a skinny teenager. He was really mad. He chased me around the bowling alley. Don't believe his intentions were good.

The man was catching up as I ran through the racks of bowling balls. So, did what seemed appropriate—and necessary—at the time. Quickly dropped a couple bowling balls in his path. Oops! Quit washing dishes that day.

Still remember his ugly face and fat tummy. Don't know if he hurt himself falling over those two bowling balls. Showed that bully how a skinny, one-eyed kid fights back. Bigger doesn't always mean "badder".

Just glad my feet were faster that day. If he had caught and squeezed me, the plastic eye would have popped out for sure. That would have been considered a strike—or maybe a split.

Clutch In, Clutch Out!

A great event happened in my freshman year at Borger Junior High School. One of the electives was Driver's Education. In Texas at that time you could get a license when you were 14. Perish that thought today. Anyway, tried signing up, but the class was full.

Shortly into the course, someone dropped out. The teacher, Mr. E.J. Grimes, finished with three of the four. That left him with time to give me individual driving instruction, so I had no distractions while learning. Mr. Grimes, one of the nicest people and father of my classmate Gary Grimes, took me and the four-door, 1958 Chevrolet for my lessons. The Chevrolet had a brake for Mr. Grimes on the passenger side. Nice green and white, as I recall. Remember, I'm three quarters of a century old. Also standard shift. That car would be a collectible today.

My Dad had not taught me to drive after the experience of accidents with my two older brothers. Yes, Robert, one was you. However, when about 12-years-old, a neighbor, Frank, did put me behind the wheel one evening. A beer drinker, he'd had a few and let me drive his manual shift Studebaker. Frank explained how to drive the car. Popped the clutch, and off we went. Chug,

chug, chug. So, that was my first experience to drive a car. Would like to own that Studebaker—believe it was a 1936—today. It would be worth some bucks.

That was my only experience until Mr. Grimes taught me how to drive correctly. He was a patient man. He probably would not be happy with me today since I tend to speed a little. Okay, a lot. Great driving record though. Just watch for the police, keep that one eye alert. Likely a better driver than most with two eyes because I'm constantly forced to look all directions. Make sense? Doesn't have to, I just know.

Well, Mr. Grimes and I would drive around the town for the hourly class. Instruction included learning to parallel park between two posts placed on a city street. Actually learned to do so without hitting the posts. Thanks to Mr. Grimes' teaching, passed the test, got my license and was off to a new world. A licensed driver at 15.

That new world led to me buying my first car, a large, four-door, 1948 Chevrolet. Purchased that for $125 with my first tax refund of $115. Told you I started working early. A nice salesman named Dean Friend sold me my first car at Rentfrow Motors. Owner was father of a high school friend and classmate, Ronnie Rentfrow.

That car was brownish/gray and built like a tank. A couple interesting incidents happened with that car. Just backing up one time, obviously not paying enough attention. Red dirt beside the road had washed out and there was a large, deep hole due to rain. All of a sudden the car came to an abrupt halt.

Unfortunately, the rear wheels had dropped into a large hole washed out by the rain. Fortunately, the bumper and part of the trunk were hanging on the other side of the hole. The wheels hung free, just spinning. Yeah, had to call a tow truck, but the car was fine. Must have been backing up trying to see with my plastic right eye.

Since that Chevrolet was built like a tank, it saved my car once again. With friends, we went driving in the country one night. My friend William Horton was following, but he fell behind in his 1951 Plymouth. While rounding a curve, slowed down a bit for William to get closer. He did. All of a sudden there was a crash into the back of my car. We pulled over.

The front of William's car hit my sturdy bumper with two big bumper guards. My trunk had one minor dent. Unfortunately, if memory is working, William had to replace the hood and two front fenders of that Plymouth. Should have bought a Chevrolet. Can't remember if I maybe did something dumb and slowed too much. Sorry, William, if that was what really happened. He was a good friend and nice fellow.

Since readers will get to read about all my work experience through the years, guess this is the place to mention my job the summer between my freshman and sophomore years. I was 15, going on 16, at the time. Sister Helen and husband C.E. Welch lived in Claude, Texas, a small town about 30 miles south of Amarillo on the main highway between Wichita Falls and Amarillo. C.E. owned a 24-hour gas station, and many overnight travelers would stop for gasoline.

Well, C.E. hired me to run the station 6 p.m. to 6 a.m. seven days a week. He worked the day shift. Let me tell you, that job provided many memories. One in particular was a woman with three young children. She stopped in around 2 a.m. one morning. Needed gas, but had no money, and wanted enough fuel to get to Amarillo. She was desperate. With tears in her eyes, she said she would have sex with me for $3 worth of gas. Since gas was about 19.9 cents per gallon at the time, that meant 15 gallons. Well, it really wasn't about the money. Or the sex.

The woman's story broke my heart, and I did the honorable thing. I gave her the gasoline, and paid from my own pocket. No sex. Anyone doing less would be a monster. And, I adore little kids. It was just one of several such stories about people down on their luck during that summer. Just hoped that woman found a better life for her and the beautiful children down the road. Such times sometimes make people better and stronger.

People with no money for gasoline occurred often. Once I traded a man gasoline for a nice Rawlings baseball glove. Other times it might be an item from their car. If I did such a transaction, I always paid for the gasoline from my own funds. Never cheated my brother-in-law.

The toughest night I had during that summer was changing eight tires on an 18-wheeler. And, we did not have the modern equipment used today. It meant breaking down the huge split rims and switching the tires. Lucky I didn't get my head knocked off when filling the tires with air. That happened to some when the split rim would fly off when filling the tire with air. Some died. I did take the precaution of placing the tire behind a steel post. If the rim came off, maybe I wouldn't lose my head. Fortunately, it never happened.

It was definitely an interesting summer job. One benefit was that my sister—like my mother—was a fabulous cook. Everyday before going to work she would prepare a fantastic meal to get me through the night. Kind of meals which should put meat on the bones, but it didn't on my 120-pound frame. Frame's not the same today with another 50 pounds from my wife's wonderful cooking.

Like I said, Claude is a small town on a main highway. It got some recognition when "Hud", starring Paul Newman, was filmed outside of town. Believe my sister still has a photo with Newman when he visited the pharmacy where she worked on the town square.

Please forgive me but memories just keep flowing, trying to get this story through my schooling. It's also necessary to quickly get them on paper. At 75, the memory may not return, necessitating interruption while it's on the surface.

Perhaps when finished this can be placed in an organized manner. Or, maybe not. Afterall, just getting these details on paper is what's important. If it doesn't make the New York Times best seller list, Oh Well! Seeing some books by politicians on the list, this should definitely hit the Top Five. Only need a publisher, and someone who appreciates a true story rather than fake news. Well, it's not fake if my memory serves me correctly. Never written fiction, at least to my recollection. Once wrote a column called "This, That, The Other" which was often humorous, but not fiction.

Wash Those Dishes, Fry Those Burgers

Okay, so I had been a student with fine grades until ninth grade, but then began working seriously washing dishes to keep the money flowing. Then came Algebra and my first educational rough spot. Until then, my math skills were great. But had never really found it necessary to study much after class. Just pay attention in class.

For me, Algebra meant studying and that was difficult with my work and what little fun time remained. No longer having my school records, it was my first memory below a B, maybe even an A. Managed to pass Algebra, but it wasn't a great grade. Would never use algebra anyway. In the 11th grade I took Geometry. It proved useful, and certainly a better grade than in algebra. General math is more useful in the financial world of newspapers. Never needed algebra—or geometry—while preparing multi-million dollar budgets. Knew how many pounds in a ton, and that was later important. Bought newsprint by the ton.

Many budget meetings were attended during my years in the newspaper business. My better-educated corporate friends were sometimes impressed. They would be punching numbers into their little calculators. Sometimes I provided the answer before they could get the numbers punched into those little devices. They wondered how that could happen. It all went back to the chalkboard competition in the early grades. After all, there are shortcuts to arithmetic. Entering high school, my goal was to graduate. Neither my parents or brothers and sisters had done so. All were certainly smart enough. Oldest sister Helen was in her senior year when she decided to get married and become a farmer's wife. Sister Joann also got married before finishing high school. Brother Robert later got his G.E.D, then a divinity degree at Baptist Bible College in Springfield, Missouri. Only one to finish college. Not to say I lost interest in school, and it was not second to my working. But it was close. Working later became part of my high school curriculum and education. Brother Billy decided to join the Army before finishing high school, and brother Jimmy decided to go to work.

One of my favorite classes was English, and one of my all-time favorite teachers was Maxine Everett. Lucky for me, as previously stated, reading was easy for me. Mrs. Everett discovered my ability to read clearly and loud enough for the class to hear.

We were into Shakespeare, and she would sometimes have me read to the class. Reading for the class certainly helped my grade. We all had a laugh one day when I was whipping through the pages of Shakespeare. Still remember: "To be, or not to be, that is the question....whether 'tis nobler in the mind to suffer the slings and arrows of outrageous fortune...". You get the picture.

One particular day while reading quickly, the passage included the word teat. Pronounced it as such, then realized it really meant tit. As I said, we all had a good laugh. At least those who understood. Funny that's one of the memories popping out of the old head.

My sophomore year was also when I went to work at the Bunavista Drive-In Theater, a few miles outside of Borger. The owner, Johnny Fagan, was a real promoter, including his dollar-a-car nights. One night he might have me in the booth selling tickets, but more often worked in the most fabulous movie theater snack bar EVER.

As indicated, Mr. Fagan was a promoter and I should mention that everything was painted pink to attract attention. Looked great, and he had a pink and white Cadillac sedan Deville to match. Still can't believe he sent me on an errand in that Cadillac. Certainly drove smoother than my Chevrolet.

Before going too far afield, let's go back to the snack bar where the real money was made. One of the great food items was the Juicy Burger, sort of like a Sloppy Joe, but better. Should have kept the recipe. Some years ago speaking with his daughter, Susan told me how it came about. I just don't remember at 75.

Anyway, it was hamburger meat and, as I recall, tomato sauce or juice and some seasonings. It would simmer in that big cooker for hours. We then used a hamburger bun not yet halved. That was sliced, in the middle, leaving it together, then spooned that delicious juicy stuff into the bun. It was a customer favorite. And mine.

Not only that, we would grill hamburgers on order, along with great chili dogs. After getting their order, customers would enter either side of the line which led to sodas, fresh popcorn and candy. We also made fresh doughnuts covered with sugar and cinnamon. Remember, everything except the candy was fresh and hot. Often, customers would eat the Juicy Burger while going through the line, and return for more. It was pure genius the way Mr. Fagan placed the kitchen, then onto other items on the snack bar. Marketing 101.

Mr. Fagan might only charge $1 a carload on a Friday night, but money was made at the snack bar. Should mention he would have a drawing on either a Friday or Saturday night for cash. The lot was filled, and in winter cars were able to have a small electric heater hanging on the driver's window to keep them warm.

That was not the only heat coming from the cars with teenagers. Maybe even adults. Many windows became fogged over. Movie didn't seem to matter.

It should also be noted that the drive-in was on a main road to Amarillo, but sort of in the country. When not $1 a carload night, it was always suspicious when there was only the driver in a car. This made the person selling tickets a tad suspicious. The driver might also be acting just a bit strange or nervous. If that was the case, another employee was alerted and someone would spot the car after it entered the lot.

Sure enough, another person—or more—may have been dumped along the fence and sneaked in the back of the property to avoid buying a ticket. Sometimes the offender would have people in the trunk and let them out after paying for one or two tickets. Many were caught. Some not.

One classmate remembered when I caught her and others sneaking into the drive-in. She wrote in my annual: "I'll never forget the time you caught us sneaking into the Drive Inn. That was a riot." She was a good friend, but died early in life. Don't remember if I charged the group when I caught them. Maybe not.

As with Mr. Darby, thanks to Johnny Fagan for allowing me to work, earn money, and also learn from his experience as a promoter. And, teaching me how to cook the Juicy Burger concoction. Sure wish I could remember that recipe. It was out-of-this-world good.

A Foot in the Door, and Drag Racing

That gets me through high school as a sophomore, and launched me to my next experience with a wonderful man and teacher, Mr. E.B. Grady. Should first point out I took a summer class before my junior year. By doing so, I was able to take Distributive Education as a junior and senior. That summer course made it possible for me to leave class at noon in order to go to work

The D.E. program helped me get my first hourly newspaper job. That foot in the door led me to a long and rewarding newspaper career. Eventually turned out to be the most important career step in my life.

Mr. Grady had formed a relationship with many businesses in Borger, and they would hire the D.E. students for part-time work. They had to agree students worked at least 15 hours a week. Mr. Grady was terrific and emphasized two important skills: Applying for a Job, and Sales.

Really wanted to work in the Borger News-Herald circulation department because it paid minimum wage of $1.10 an hour. However, at the school year beginning, they had no openings. So, went to work stocking for Levine's, a department store, at 50 cents an hour. Totally overjoyed shortly afterwards when a job came open at the Borger News-Herald, and joined other D. E. students.

This foot-in-the-door later led me into what became a career. While in circulation, the job included removing newspapers as they came off an old press. The process was known as hot metal, rather than offset.

A page was setup in lead, and a lead plate was then made to fit on the press cylinders. The new guy was normally the person who got to perform the unpopular job of removing the newspapers as they came off the press folder. It required bending over and removing the papers, 25 or 50 at a time, depending on page count. The press automatically kicked out a "turn" at 25 or 50, and I would grab the turn, shake it down, and stack it on a table. They were then stacked in a cart by another person and taken to the mailroom to be tied in bundles for distribution to carriers.

While truly liking pressmen Buck Bonds and Jimmy Banks, they would irritate me at times by cranking the press to full speed. It was extremely difficult to grab the turn, shake it down and stack it before the newspapers would roll off the press onto the floor. Okay fellows, you're forgiven for those times while you were laughing.

In circulation we would also be assigned to knock doors and sell subscriptions, sometimes in towns 80 miles away. While towns such as Dumas (40 miles) and Perryton (80 miles) had no daily newspaper, it could still be a difficult sell. It certainly polished my sales skills.

After soliciting in Perryton one day, not one person was convinced to subscribe. After returning, my circulation manager

Dean Preston questioned my effort. Really tried, knocked a lot of doors, but could not get a subscriber. But, Dean was great to me. When I became sports editor a few years later, he would cover football games. We covered a large area with about 13 high schools. Anyone working at the newspaper who enjoyed sports and could put words together was recruited to cover games.

A few years after, Dean joined the news staff at the Pueblo Chieftain in Colorado. He enjoyed writing, and believe he had an English degree. Another one of the truly nice people during my newspaper years. Unfortunately, he is one of my friends who have passed.

Another of our jobs in circulation was counting and tying out bundles (with copper wire or twine) to be distributed to newspaper carriers. This prior to all the advertising circulars now distribute in newspapers. If the newspaper was more than 16 pages, it required an additional run because of press capacity.

On Sundays, there would be an extra section and Sunday comics. The extra section had to be run on the press prior to the main front section. Two or three of us would go in early on Saturday night, then insert color comics into that section. Those comics were printed elsewhere, and shipped to the News-Herald.

Without seeing, it is difficult to visualize the fast hand coordination of those of us doing that inserting. Imagine a stack of newspaper sections and a stack of comics side-by-side. Now, imagine fast hands placing the comics into the section. It was necessary to lift the section into half, and speed of the comics hitting it would automatically carry while the next section was grabbed for the next comic section. It was impressive.

My best and lifetime friend Kenneth Duncan and I were both fast. So was Roy Jones. We could insert 2,500 or so an hour. Maybe even more. Large newspapers may have used inserting machines. Smaller newspapers didn't normally use them until the large volume of preprints came along years later.

Before going further, thank you E.B. Grady for helping get me placed at the Borger News-Herald. I was president of our Distributive Education class my senior year, and had bought a new 1961 Ford, financed of course. By that time, my '48 Chevrolet had thrown a rod. It was replaced by a white 1951 Ford hardtop, followed by a 1954 green Ford, then the new 1961 Ford. Moving up in the world of flashy cars. Nice green.

Drag racing was in my blood by my junior year. My 1954 Ford was fast and beat others of the same year. Except for a four-door 1954 Ford owned by Larry Fletcher. Whipped him off the line, but then he passed and won. Still don't believe his motor was stock. Larry is the brother of Troy, a good friend since we worked together at the Borger News-Herald. Troy, a really great guy, later had his own barber shop. He cut my hair as long as I lived in Borger. A good barber, too. Brother Charlie—-who recently passed—was also a fine fellow.

Oh, should mention at this point the trophies won for my category at the new Amarillo drag strip. My little '54 Ford was fast off the line. My nemesis was a 1959 Ford pickup from, I believe, Clovis, N.M. Never beat him when racing in the finals. Felt he didn't have a stock six-cylinder, but it was not worth the $75 (as I recall) fee to have his engine broken down to check. Trophy wasn't worth $75 to me. Besides, I didn't have the $75.

Along with that fast '54, my talent was being quick off the starting line, and changing gears. That quickness made it nearly impossible to tell when going from low to second, and second to high. Still have quick reactions while driving, even at my advanced age. Although, my car now has an automatic transmission. With the old knees, that's a good thing.

While on the subject, might as well let you know we had quarter miles marked off in several locations surrounding Borger. We always left one person posted to watch for the Highway Patrol. That person would honk a horn if a patrol car was spotted. We all suddenly disappeared down the road, driving normal speed. Highway Patrol never caught us drag racing, at least when I was at one of these fun competitions.

Well, Mr. Grady decided to take me and Frank Gunn to the state Distributive Education competition in Galveston at Texas' southern tip. He asked if we could take my new Ford, which we did. Didn't bother him that I would be driving with only one eye. Seems about 800 or 900 students from throughout Texas attended, competing in the contests.

Those of us participating in the Job Application contest were interviewed by, as I recall, two businessmen for a particular job. While not winning, I did place—somewhere. At 75, I just don't remember how high—or low. What a great experience, and always did well in job interviews throughout my career. Sales, too. Thanks to pointers from Mr. Grady.

There are still some Distributive Education programs in high schools. They can certainly help some students down the path to a fine career. Would also say the same about the Diversified Occupation (D.O.) programs. At that time at least, D.O. was for students interested in jobs with other skills, such as becoming an automobile mechanic. They can lead to good jobs—and careers. Not everyone can, or want, to be a bank president.

There you have it. Graduated high school, May, 1961. Let me be clear, I am a strong believer in education. Obviously can't say my approach would be the best for all students, but it worked for me. There is no substitute for teaching and learning the basics. They give you a foot up in life and the world. During my career, those basics were key to huge multi-million dollar budgets, and successfully being in charge of newspapers. And groups of newspapers.

Key People in My Life

At this point, let me just say many of us have people who played a big role in what success we had in life. Without doubt, my parents top the list. In mine, I would at this point like to acknowledge some other very important people you will read about later in this book. They all contributed to what was an extremely satisfying career. One which I had never thought about—or dreamed about—while growing up in my hometown of Borger, Texas. Those playing such a role follow:

EIGHTH GRADE TYPING TEACHER; This is horrible but I can't remember her name. To keep me from associating with the wrong crowd, she placed me in a semester typing class. That class was a key to my long newspaper career. Without that introductory class to typing, it's almost certain my career would have been something different.

E.B. GRADY—Borger High School Distributive Education teacher during my junior and senior years. He was the person responsible for me getting a job in the circulation department of my hometown newspaper, the Borger News Herald. Not only that, he cultivated my skills in job application and sales. Both were extremely important skills. He was a sweet man and wonderful teacher.

WAYNE LANHAM & FRED WORTHAM—These two gentleman somehow realized I had skills beyond working in the circulation department and doing janitorial work at night at the newspaper. Mr. Lanham, advertising director, and Mr. Wortham, city editor, sat me down one day. Mr. Lanham offered me a job in sales, and Mr. Wortham wanted to hire me as a reporter. They saw something in me that I had not at that point recognized. During my first year at Frank Phillips Junior College, I became a reporter. That was the first step to an almost 50-year career as a reporter, editor, publisher and supervisor of groups of newspapers.

To me, it was an amazing and important event.

PHILIP E. SWIFT: When I left Texas and moved to California, Mr. Swift, in charge of about 11 daily Scripps League Newspapers, hired me as a reporter for the South Lake Tahoe Tribune. A wonderful man, he was responsible for me becoming a daily newspaper editor and 18-year employee of Scripps League. A highly intelligent man and great friend to me. Thought so highly of Mr. Swift that we named our son after him.

BARRY SCRIPPS—Son of Ed and Betty Scripps, we became friends when I was a reporter and he was in sales for the Napa Register. We have been friends for more than 50 years. When the Scripps owners divided the newspapers, Barry became in charge of the Scripps League. He named me to my first publisher job in Flat River, Missouri in 1978. I left that job to run a division of newspapers for Park Communications. Barry later hired me as publisher for a Scripps newspaper in Santa Maria, Calif. It was important he named me to my first publisher's job, as well as being a good friend. Exceptionally nice man.

ALLEN MEATH—Mr. Meath hired me from my first publisher's job to be in charge of a division of newspapers for Park

Communication. I worked out of their headquarters in Ithaca, N.Y. and supervised newspapers in five states. Fine man, friend, and a great sense of humor. It surprised me to be hired for such a job after only five years as a publisher, but he and others at Park recognized my skills at making money as a publisher, and still produce good newspapers. It was fun, and a great learning experience for me.

ROBERT (BOB) JELENIC—Bob first hired me as publisher when he was in charge of Ingersoll Newspapers. Ingersoll was later bought by Journal Register Co. where Bob ran the company. He first hired me to run the Anderson (Indiana) Herald-Bulletin. That newspaper was sold, and Bob later hired me as publisher in Fall River, MA. He was a terrific guy, boss and friend for years. While he is deceased, he provided me with great opportunities, nice salaries, and a job which led me to retirement. While he wanted newspapers to make money, he also insisted they produce quality products and insisted they have local content, especially sports coverage. His trust in me will not be forgotten.

Here I Come!

So, what to do with my life, having accomplished my goal of graduating high school. That was the big question, and knew there would always be a need for teachers. Many chose that path, and short of a better goal, thought that might be okay. Hey, teachers were off three months in the summer during those days.

Entering local Frank Phillips Junior College, Mrs. Everett (my sophomore English teacher) was then teaching a journalism class at Frank Phillips. Okay, a favorite teacher, and maybe an easy class. Certainly had no thought of being a journalist. By scheduling classes at the right time, I was also able to continue working in the newspaper circulation department. In order to get to 40 hours a week, the nightly newspaper janitorial job was added to my schedule. Sweep, mop, empty trash cans. Nice, making more money to pay for that new Ford.

Taking Mrs. Everett's class proved to be the launching pad for my journalism career. One day, Borger News-Herald Advertising Manager Wayne Lanham and City Editor Fred Wortham said they would like to speak with me. Never, ever, could I have imagined what was about to take place.

Mr. Lanham said he and Mr. Wortham had been discussing me. He wanted to hire me as an advertising salesman. Mr. Wortham wanted to hire me as a reporter. Could have knocked me over with a feather. They asked me to think about it and let them know if I was interested.

Interested? Are you kidding me? From hustling in the mailroom and mopping floors to a real 40-hour job? While really liking both of them, it just seemed like being a reporter held a bit more challenge. Choosing to become a reporter was a judicious decision. Also covered and wrote sports. This from a guy who only played Little League as a youngster.

Working during high school, no time for sports. Besides, my parents wouldn't let me try out for football because of my one eye. Too skinny anyway, and the plastic eye might have popped out if I got hit in the helmet. Not fond of pain. If playing offensive end, it would have to be the right end so I could see the pass coming with my left eye. Might not have worked out so well. Certainly would have a stiff neck—and pain in other body locations.

How and why did the two of them want me to work in their departments? Believe it boiled down to my hard work and their belief I possessed skills to do the job. Thanks, gentlemen, for your faith and ability to assess my potential. Never had that thought entered my mind. Turned out they were both right. My positions as reporter, editor and publisher turned out fine, and my sales skills were important as a publisher. Sales skills are not only useful in selling a product, but in selling yourself to others.

Spent almost two years as a reporter, and also covered sports. Then, it was off to West State College located in Canyon, about

70 miles away. Okay, going bigtime, the college name plastered over the back window of that 1961 Ford. Almost everyone with a car had their college/university logo on the rear window. Guess it meant we were smart enough for college.

Troy Martin was owner and publisher of the Canyon News, a weekly paper serving the college town. He looked at my background and hired me as sports editor to cover West Texas. Not only that, he found out I had worked in circulation and could insert newspapers very fast.

When resigning, he told me he wished he could afford to hire me again in the future. He believed I had a bright future ahead in newspapers. He was right. Once again, someone realized my talent. While just trying to get along by working, it became obvious there was a future for me in reporting. Mr. Martin was an interesting, nice man and very supportive.

The Canyon News was one of the early offset newspapers. We would put it together on Tuesdays. Then, I would drive the pages about 30 miles to have it printed. I would return with two sections of about 3,500 each around 2 a.m., and would insert them for Wednesday distribution. Needless to say, it meant not being too alert in morning classes.

Well, made it through the first semester with about 12 credits. Fifteen or 16 credits were considered a full load. Not too great, but made a decision to enroll second semester.

Let me also mention that in addition to working for the newspaper, I also kept play-by-play for West Texas football home games. A busy fellow. Covering West Texas was fun because that was the year a small running back, "Pistol Pete" Pedro, from Lynn, MA was one of—maybe first—of the top players in rushing for the country. Probably only about 165 pounds, he was exciting to watch. Joe Kerbel was the coach.

Yes, maybe education was taking a backseat to work. My Dad had borrowed $500 from the Phillips Credit Union to help with my school expenses. While appreciated, that bothered me.

Abilene, Abilene

That's when Mike Wester and the Abilene Reporter-News job came into my life. My education with schools was over, and was off with my one eye open to a new world. Being single and the new man on the sports staff, many weekends were spent covering the summer golf tournaments. That meant traveling a bit. It seemed every town within 80 miles of Abilene had a tournament during the summer.

One of those golfers was Rives McBee, a school teacher who could really hit the ball, winning a number of tournaments. He later turned pro. Believe he set a one round record of 64 in a major 1966 PGA tournament at San Francisco.

With so many golf tournaments around Abilene, a number of fellows won the various tournaments. While attending one of those, a really good golfer took me aside, seeking my opinion. It was match play, and a friend and fellow golfer asked the man to let him win. I told him definitely not to throw the match. Sure enough, the golfer seeking my advice kicked butt, took the tourney and won a set of golf clubs as the winner. Glad he listened and won. Certainly would have wondered had he lost. Honesty is always first with me.

While in Abilene, got to meet former Washington Redskins quarterback Sammy Baugh. He didn't seem all that big to have played quarterback. He was known as Slingin' Sammy Baugh. Passing wasn't as big in professional football during those days. So Baugh was unique with his passing talent. He's in the NFL Hall of Fame.

Should also mention an invitation to view the Astrodome being built for the Houston Colt .45s. That was the first of its kind and it was huge. Construction began in 1962 and was completed in 1965.

The Astrodome was previewed for newspaper and broadcast folks. A demonstration for these news people and others showed it was impossible to hit the roof of the facility with a baseball. That was a great event for me, and singer Anita Bryant was at a dinner. Schlitz helped us along with the beer. Hadn't given that a thought for years until writing this little offering for my children. Yep, still got memories lingering in the old mind. Keeping my one eye on the world.

Back to Home and Moving On

After about six months at the Abilene Reporter-News, Fred Wortham came into my life once again. The sports editor's job was vacant. He wanted to hire me for the spot back in my hometown of Borger. Seemed like the right thing to do, so returned to my hometown. Interesting when you perform well for an employer, they sometimes want to hire you again once you're gone. Happened to me four times in my career. Honesty, common sense, hard work, and the ability to do to the job are key.

Spent about nine months as sports editor, but then another life-changing event happened. There was this fine looking girl who worked in accounting. We dated, decided to get married. Off we went to Clayton, N.M. with sister Joann and her husband, Harold Cobb, in my new bronze, 1965 fastback Mustang. Wish that car still belonged to me.

Previously had ordered a yellow, white interior Mustang from the factory at a dealer in a neighboring town. Placed a $50 deposit. Ford went on strike, and didn't know how long that would last. Local dealer, Bob Johnson Ford, had the fastback available, so I bought. My deposit was not returned. If that happened today, that money would be returned. Not my fault

Ford went on strike, seems for about six weeks. That dealer's no longer in business.

Anyway, we found a Justice of the Peace and he agreed to go to the courthouse, get the paperwork and perform the ceremony. The other thing I remember is that he had gout, a crying baby, and wife serving as a witness to the ceremony. It was on a Sunday, and he performed the wedding at his home. Paid him, just don't remember the cost. No champagne afterwards, maybe an A&W root beer.

We made the return trip to Borger. Sure enough, the sheets on our bed had been short-sheeted, and there was rice in the bed. That was a custom during those days. Maybe still today.

The new wife had a grandmother in San Francisco. We decided California was our future, so bought an enclosed trailer about the size of a U-Haul, and gave Fred Wortham the bad news. He was very disappointed I was leaving. Felt bad, but somehow knew another challenge awaited me. Turned out to be the right decision to launch my career.

Everyone told me I was a good writer, so had no fear about finding a job. My brother Jimmy painted the trailer, and we got a hitch for my 1965 Ford Mustang. Never been there, but California here we come.

What the heck, new wife, a few years experience as a reporter, sports editor, and desire for a new experience. Afterall, Horace Greeley had said, "go west young man." He was very wise. But, he had taken the saying from John B.L. Sole, although most have attributed it to Horace Greeley through the years. No matter, I heeded the advice.

At that time, every car was stopped and checked before entering California. The man asked what we had in the trailer. Explained it was just our household goods. He wanted to see it, but let him know that was a bad idea because it was packed. He insisted. Before leaving Texas I had sprayed WD-40 in a lock on each side of the fold down rear gate. Handing him one key, I took the other.

The man grabbed the lock, and he was rewarded with greasy hands. I told him we needed to open very carefully. My suspicion to this day is that he believed something illegal was in that trailer. There wasn't.

We barely opened the gate. Clothing and household items began to make their exit. Okay, he said, close the gate. He should have been able to recognize an honest Texan. Probably the Buddy Holly glasses made him suspicious. Maybe he just didn't want any prohibited fruit from entering California, bringing ruinous pests to the many orchards in the state.

In my infinite wisdom, thought it would be nice to drive through Yosemite, then to San Francisco. Never considered while driving east of the mountain range in Nevada that the pass to California would be closed because of snow. Of course I had never been to California, and actually knew little about the state. Realized they had lots of newspapers. Opportunity and new challenges were just waiting for me in the Golden State. It was early May, 1965.

That meant we needed to go north to Carson City, and up the mountain to South Lake Tahoe where we spent the night. Thought it was a beautiful and special place. Not a thought that a few weeks later this Texas boy would be returning as a reporter for the South Lake Tahoe Tribune.

Hello, California

Driving on Highway 50 from South Lake Tahoe, through Placerville, and south toward Sacramento offered some of the most gorgeous sites for my first time in California. Beautiful green, rolling hills. It's been years since last traveling that route, but even then housing was springing up along the hills. Certainly many more today.

Then we rolled along into San Francisco with clean streets compared to a mess today in current areas with litter from druggies and the homeless. A sad difference, but still a beautiful City by The Bay. Today, it can also lay claim to being home to—unfortunately—U.S. Speaker of the House Nancy Pelosi. While writing this she had another of her infamous flubs, wishing news media a Happy Thanksgiving. She meant to say Happy Valentine's Day. It's frightening to understand she is third in line after the U.S. President.

Winding through on Highway 101, we turned off, finally reaching the wife's grandmother near the famed Cow Palace. Then the challenge really got underway. Finding a job meant becoming acquainted with the state's newspapers. It took a bit longer than expected for this Texas boy. Seemed the first order of business was to seek out newspapers, including placing an advertisement in the San Francisco Examiner and Chronicle. Really, who wouldn't want to hire me?

That didn't work out so well, and my inexperience outside of Texas was showing. No one from a newspaper responded, but did receive a couple calls from hookers. Yeah, that's a prostitute. They were seeking work, not offering me a job. Kindly explained I had no interest in their offerings. Why would they believe a man seeking employment would have money for their type entertainment anyway? Perhaps they believed it would help me forget about not having a job.

Their calls did break the monotony of job hunting. They had an interesting sales pitch. And, they could read the newspaper. My first experience with the California entertainment industry. Newly married, I didn't need it.

It was then I discovered the California Newspaper Publishers Association in Sacramento. The CNPA not only listed openings in newspapers, but would also place my advertisement. For free.

After about a month, my Dad became worried about my unemployment. He informed me that Fred Wortham would accept me in my Texas hometown—again—as sports editor. Explained I would keep looking in California. A great decision on my part. Someone surely wanted—and needed—a talented young reporter. Even though I didn't have a college degree. I did have experience, and that was accepted—if not preferred—by some during that era. Maybe even today.

Then I received a response, interviewed, and was hired at the San Leandro Times in the East Bay. At the same time, fate showed its beautiful head. Ross Game, editor at the Napa Register, said he would like me to come for an interview. Had a wisdom tooth yanked in the morning, then drove to Napa for the interview with Mr. Game and a gentleman named Philip E. Swift. Mr. Swift oversaw a number of newspapers for the Scripps League of Newspapers.

Mr. Swift was a special man and became a key to 18 years of my success as I moved up the ladder with Scripps League of Newspapers. Thought so highly of him that my second wife, Janice, and I named our first child, Philip, after him. Never forget, Mr. and Mrs. Swift later sent us a nice baptismal outfit for our son in Logan, Utah. Mr. Swift had lived in Logan, and knew the Presbyterian minister Miner Bruner, who performed our wedding ceremony.

The interview with Mr. Swift and Mr. Game was pretty amazing as I had a big hole from the tooth being pulled that morning. Uh oh, it was leaking blood, so just sucked it down and kept talking. Just glad they were across the desk from me. Bad breath surely would have cost me the job. After about an hour, Mr. Swift said he and Mr. Game would like to check my references with Fred Wortham and get back to me the next day.

Explained that would not be possible since I was to begin work in San Leandro the next day. Mr. Swift asked if I could return in an hour, and I agreed. Upon my return, Mr. Swift said Mr. Wortham thought I should get in my Mustang, head for South Lake Tahoe, and become a reporter for the South Lake Tahoe Tribune, owned by Scripps League. Wow, my second job offer in a California newspaper. Blessings were abundant.

Mr. Swift said the job would pay $100 a week. While difficult to believe even today, I explained my salary was more than that when leaving Texas. Afterall, my weekly salary was $100, but collected another $10 a week from phoning in sports results to the Amarillo Globe-News. How could I be so brazen? Well, there was the other job in San Leandro and I needed the other $10 a week. Besides, Lake Tahoe was an expensive place to live.

Mr. Swift, a mild-mannered gentleman from Missouri, then told me they would give me $110 a week. Here we come South Lake Tahoe. A master at understanding people, he knew I had been out of work for over a month. He then asked if he could give me a loan to help get me started. Thanked him, but said we would be fine. Hey, after all, we had enough money for food, gas, and deposit on an apartment. Well, maybe a bit more. Just not enough for gambling at the casinos.

Beautiful South Lake Tahoe

Working at South Lake Tahoe in 1965 provided me with great opportunities on a small news staff. Fires, auto accidents and airplane crashes, while tragic, allowed me to cut my teeth on reporting hard news. Not only that, each of us on the small staff carried a camera. Never done that before, but it just became an extension of my hands.

The camera was a Yashica 120. Twelve nice big negatives to a roll of film. As reporters, we also did our film developing, and printing screened prints for publication. Our chemicals allowed us to develop film "hot", printing a screened print from wet negatives in about five minutes. Suppose a "real" photographer would cringe at such. However, we just needed to produce a newspaper, and get onto the next one.

At that time South Lake Tahoe was not an incorporated city, but voted to become so while I was there. My beat included the El Dorado County Sheriff's Department. Headquarters were in Placerville, but they had a substation across from our newspaper. Becoming friends with the officers and personnel was easy, and key to my success. Did the same with the California Highway Patrol lieutenant in charge and those officers. One of my strengths has always been making friends easily, and dealing with people.

As a result of making these important contacts, when there were fires or accidents, I was often the first call from the dispatcher after officers and ambulances were dispatched to emergencies. That meant being one of the first on the scene. It provided opportunity for great photos. Became quite the photographer. As a service, I would print photos for the Sheriff's Office and CHP when requested. Receiving those emergency calls day and night certainly helped the Tribune stomp big city competitors in coverage.

Didn't know the fire department as well, but received emergency fire calls from the sheriff's office. One day there was a call about a fire. The fire station was about three blocks from the Tribune offices. Grabbed my camera, hopped in my Mustang, driving in the middle turn lane, just behind the fire truck.

We sped a couple miles to the fire. Hopping out with my camera, a fireman quickly stopped me. The fireman was visibly upset. In other words, he was mad. He told me I wasn't supposed to follow so close to the fire truck. Promptly informed him if they had gotten out of my way, I wouldn't have been following. That ended the discussion. He fought the fire, and I shot the photos.

Both had our jobs to do.

That story's for my friend (?) from New Jersey, a retired fire chief or some such title. Hey, he worked for a city little more than a square mile, across from New York City. Sure they didn't even have a middle lane for a photographer to rush to a fire. Probably just pulled the hose along the street to the fire. This could mean I don't get invited to his house for coffee and doughnuts every

Monday morning. And his sort-of handle bar mustache may now turn down rather than up. Sorry pal, had to do it.

The Tribune relied almost entirely on local news, so we needed photos each day. One of the best sources were schools, so made those important contacts. If we needed a photo, just had to contact a school. They always had something happening, and it also helped with readership. Newspapers today fail to realize the benefit of covering school activities. The newspaper was recognized for its school coverage by the state teachers association.

Importance of making friends in the right places has been my approach throughout my career. It always paid huge dividends.

At 6,250 feet, South Lake Tahoe presented a challenge, especially for some smaller airplanes. To get out of the basin, it was sometimes necessary for pilots to crisscross back and forth to gain altitude and over the tall Sierra mountain range. Unfortunately, some pilots were loaded (literally), and so were the airplanes. That resulted in airplane crashes.

While it's been many years, seems during my time at South Tahoe, over 20 crashes claimed somewhere around 19 lives. That may sound high, but I remember photographing many, two of the crashes right at the south shore claiming four lives each. The numbers could have been even higher, but that was around 50 years ago.

One crash was on takeoff at the South Tahoe Airport. It was one of the worst. Received the call, and rushed to the scene, and had to run in—probably a mile—from Highway 50. When I got to the site, the small airplane had burned. So had grass around a large area. There was a very bad smell. Four people had died in the crash. It was the only time I was ever left feeling nauseous while covering an event. Well, except listening to some politicians.

Another memorable crash occurred as a twin-engine plane was flying from the north over the lake for runway approach. The young pilot—believe he was 22—lost both engines. Just as he approached Highway 50 which ran along the lake's south shore, he was able to get one engine started again. As I recall, the engine torqued, flipped the plane, and crashed upside down a short distance from Highway 50.

It was dark when arriving shortly after emergency personnel. The plane carried four passengers and the pilot. One of my sad memories occurred as they brought the lone survivor, a man, through the rear. The man was conscious and said he thought his leg was broken. Sadly, he lost both legs and one arm. Obviously, he was in shock.

The airplane was owned by an electric company from San Jose, California. Seems I was the only photographer shooting shortly after the crash. It certainly seemed the case when insurance folks came to my office seeking copies of the crash photos. Since I rarely asked for overtime because of shooting fires and accidents, my boss allowed me to sell photos sought by insurance companies for these tragedies. No concern about overtime. Covering exciting news and gaining valuable experience were more important.

One insurance fellow wanted copies and ask the charge. I explained cost of proof sheets of each shot, and for 8x10s. Seems it was about $75 for a proof sheet of 12, and $50 for an 8x10. The man told me that was highway robbery. While that may be true, availability and demand helped determine the price. Just ask anyone with the only copy, or a product not available otherwise.

As he had pointed out, mine were the only photos. Stated I was busy, and if he wasn't interested he should leave. He paid the price. It was a small price for a lawsuit in the millions. Mine were the only photos of the airplane and emergency personnel shortly after the crash. They also showed the survivor being removed from the airplane.

If memory serves me correctly, there was a faulty part—won't mention the company—and the survivor received around $13 million. Seems it was a record settlement for such an event at the time. Believe the survivor owned the electric company and the airplane. Any newspapers with those stories have long since disappeared from my boxes. For me, it was just go onto the next story. That was my job.

While at Tahoe, I got my literal fire baptism while covering a forest fire on the southwest side of the lake. Being a gung ho reporter-photographer, I charged in along with firefighters. Didn't matter that I had a white shirt, black pants, shoes and tie. Just needed to get to the fire for those photos.

Well, the Forest Service had called in for an airplane drop. There I was in just the right spot for the pink liquid to cover me completely. Fortunately, I took a shot and quickly covered the camera. Looked real cute covered in that sticky pink stuff. But, I got the photos.

Not All Fires, Blood and Death

Living at South Lake Tahoe during those times was not all fires, blood and death. Lake Tahoe is split with California on the west, and Nevada on the east. Yeah, they split a lake between two states. At the state line, Harrah's and Harvey's had casinos. Sahara-Tahoe, then owned by Del Webb, had recently opened. Barney's was another small club next to Harrah's. That was all the casinos located at the South Shore.

Not only did folks come for the gambling, but it was the mid-1960s and some of the most famous entertainers in the world appeared in the showrooms. The Tahoe Tribune published a weekly entertainment guide, and it was my job to put it together. Also chose which headline entertainer's photo would be placed on the cover each week. Yes, that meant a little competition between the three casino's public relations people for that spot.

And, I was nearly always invited to the openings with premium seats, often down front. The greats such as Dean Martin, Sammy Davis, Milton Berle and others were headliners. Phyllis Diller was talking about her husband, Fang, at the Sahara Tahoe. I remember her standing on a ladder greeting people after the show. Oh, should also mention the talented Don Rickles. Yep, got to see them all.

Still a skinny fellow with Buddy Holly glasses, one memory was getting very red-faced at a Mitzi Gaynor performance in Harrah's South Shore Room. That night we had dinner, and were front row, center stage. Mitzi was beautiful and had a fantastic set of legs. She was on stage dancing and singing right in front of me.

Sitting with my plastic eye threatening to pop out, she bent over and asked if I liked what I saw, and, "what are you doing after the show big fella'?" You probably could have lit a cigarette off my face it was so red and hot. It didn't help that the room was dark, and they shined the spotlight on me when Mitzi spoke to me. Sure she never thought of me after that moment. But sure thought about her.

It would be a crime not to mention the great Wayne Newton. When we arrived at South Tahoe, he was performing with his brother in Harrah's lounge. He was a marvelous performer, and it wasn't long before he moved to the South Shore Room. He dropped his brother from his act. Newton was extremely talented, and had one huge hit record, "Danke Schoen". He became a major, long-running act in Las Vegas for many years, and became known as Mr. Las Vegas. He still performs.

It was great fun working with and becoming friends with the public relations folks. Harry Matte from Harrah's was among the best in the business, and we became good friends. Another time worth recalling was being invited with my wife and the PR man to visit with Liberace after his show. The PR man took us to Liberace's suite at the Sahara-Tahoe. We had drinks and visited for about 30 minutes. Not only was Liberace talented, but he was very gracious to us. Benefit of being in the right job at the right time. Geez, didn't even ask him for an autograph.

Another time, Harvey's public relations man invited me to lunch with Maury Wills, the great Los Angeles Dodgers shortstop. That was after Wills set a record 104 stolen bases in 1962, batting .299 that year. He was also the National League's Most Valuable Player. Wills was a seven time All-Star, and played outstanding in three World Series, if memory serves me correctly.

Wills also supplemented his baseball income by singing and performing instrumentally with clubs and occasionally television appearances. He was known for his banjo talent. Surely, he must have felt privileged to have lunch with a talkative, one-eyed reporter who hailed from Texas. Still have the baseball he signed for me. Thanks, Maury.

Hello, Dolly

Gonna' jump ahead one more time, in a return to Harrah's South Shore Room years later. If memory serves me correctly, it was probably in 1976 or 1977. Again as guests of Harrah's, we were down front, across from a radio personality and his wife.

Doug Kershaw, the Crazy Cajun Fiddler, was the headline act. Dolly Parton played second fiddle, so-to-speak. The PR person asked if we would be interested in visiting Dolly in her dressing room after the show. Well, duh! Did I have to think about that? Uh, no.

It's been said by many over the years, but what you see is what you get with Dolly. With us, she was just her down-home, bubbly self. We visited about 20 minutes. All of sudden Doug Kershaw, likely feeling a bit left out, came to Dolly's dressing room. Now an opportunity to visit with both.

My second wonderful wife and I still have the photo with Dolly hiding somewhere in one of many boxes. Doug Kershaw's not in the photo. Sorry old buddy, Dolly has a better..um...smile. Perhaps one day we can dig through that disaster area we call the garage and find that photo. Those boxes may also have spiders and snakes, like in the song. Maybe hang that Tennessee girl's beautiful face—and boobs—alongside our western paintings. She would not sit down during the visit. Said she would bust her britches. Heard her use that line since, but it's probably true.

Perhaps I should have the photo copied, autograph it, and send it to Dolly so she can see how well she's weathered all those years. Me, perhaps not so much. But I did get a new plastic eye.

Still can't see any better.

After returning home, I wrote a short review and said it would probably be one of the last times Dolly ever played second fiddle to anyone on stage. It was. That's when she hit the bigtime. Marvelous and highly successful, intelligent lady. The rest is history. Everyone knows Dolly Parton for singing, songwriting, acting, and creating Dollywood. Her net worth is....BIG.

While on the subject of pretty ladies with those attractive attachments, it would seem wrong not to mention my encounter with a famous San Francisco topless dancer—Carol Doda. In the mid-'60s, she delighted patrons at the Condor Club. Seems there may have been a large likeness sign out front to attract customers. She became a legend after having her breasts enhanced from a mere 34 to 44. Those certainly drew crowds and she performed into the 1980s.

There was a press club for media types at South Lake Tahoe, and I happened to be the president. Carol Doda was in town, so we invited her to a luncheon. That drew a crowd of our members, and she brought along T-shirts showing her face and image of her enhancements. Shirt probably cost about $10, but don't remember exactly. Being president of the club, she may have given it to me free.

Carol did not strip or perform her nightclub act for the group, just so you know. Didn't need to. Her appearance and talking with the tongue-tied fellows was enough. My plastic eye remained in place, even when she posed with me for a photo. That photo has since disappeared.

One memory is wearing that T-shirt to bed as a nightshirt for years. It was of a soft cotton, and large (the shirt) enough to be comfortable. Hey, everyone needs a covering to stay warm at night. Washed and wore that shirt until it became too holey. Did the wife laugh at me? Most likely. Carol was beautiful and sweet to visit with our group. She died in 2015 at age 78.

The Sacramento Bee was a large newspaper serving Northern California, including Lake Tahoe. They had a nice man named John Murphy as their South Lake Tahoe correspondent. We became friends, covering the same fires and accidents.

Sure, I was always first to the scene because his little yellow Sacramento Bee Ford Falcon couldn't keep pace with my Mustang. Don't remember him being notified by the sheriff's office either. He was a really swell fellow, and did a fine job for the Bee. Can't understand why, but he eventually moved to Alaska.

Too cold for me.

After working at the Tribune a little over a year, the Bee decided to place a correspondent at the North Shore. John Murphy was accepting that job and asked if I would be interested in being their South Shore correspondent. After all, they provided him a car and paid for using his camera. Salary was also more. They hired me, I gave notice at the Tribune, and went to Texas on vacation.

Upon my return, my managing editor, Frank Gordon, gave notice. Being brash, with nothing to lose, informed the Tribune publisher I would stay if he would give me Frank's job. He said he would need to think about it and call his boss, Phil Swift, in Napa. He did, then told me they would try me with the title of city editor for three months. If that worked, then I could be managing editor. Looking for an opportunity and up to the challenge, I agreed and got the other title after three months. Must have been about 23 at the time.

Should also mention that Frank, a native of the Napa Valley, was later my wire editor when I became managing editor in Napa. He was fast, and a talented fellow. One memorable news judgment disagreement came the day Elvis Presley died. While reading the UPI wire in Napa the story of his death came across. It was August 16, 1977.

Turned to Frank and told him the sad news, and that he had his lead for the next day's Napa Register. He said the story should go inside the newspaper. Being a fan of Elvis, I informed him it would be the biggest story for days. Needless to say, we placed it as the lead story in the next day's newspaper.

It goes without saying I was right, and Elvis has been in the news ever since. Recognizing important news stories has always been my strong forte. Elvis will always be in the house, as they often note. Fortunately, my wife and I got to see him perform. May have been earlier that year at the Cow Palace in San Francisco. It could have been 1976.

Along with millions, I was an Elvis fan and still have a large collection of his records. He was a talented entertainer with a distinct and marvelous voice. The music world—especially Rock and Roll—changed forever when Elvis hit the scene.

Keeping Reporters off Their Ass

The Tahoe Tribune was a small, five-day publication. As a result, pay was low and we always had trouble keeping a full staff. My promotion to managing editor meant hiring another reporter. We found some excellent talent. It was challenging to put out a daily newspaper with almost entirely local content. The Tribune did subscribe to the UPI radio wire, but it carried mostly short stories. UPI was used sparingly, and the stories were brief.

After a year and a half as managing editor, the idea of devoting a page to each of our newspaper's departments during National Newspaper Week seemed a good idea. That was assigned to a reporter, and he chose the copy and photos for the pages.

The Tribune had a composing foreman who would put the type and photos together. A favorite of the publisher, he would push the pages to the press room at times without the news department checking for errors. And, to make sure our page layout was followed.

Well, my reporter did the page of photos and copy for the editorial department. It was finished, shipped to the press room, and I never saw the finished product. My reporter, like me, had a sense of humor. Under my photo, he had outlined my duties. In part of my photo's cutline, he noted, "keeping reporters off their ass" was part of my duties.

Whoops! While true and humorous, it was not appropriate for the cutline. He was just having fun, intending for it to be changed before shipped for printing. That did not happen.

When returning from lunch, the publisher was waiting for me. "How could you do such a thing," he asked. Let him know I had no idea what he was talking about. He then told me about the cutline describing my duties. He allowed about 1,500 newspapers to be sent for distribution "to teach you a lesson." Well, that was certainly a poor decision. Since he felt that way, he could have tossed those newspapers and had me pay the cost. That would have been a lesson.

Informed the publisher that I never saw the page or cutline because the composing foreman, as he often did, sent it to the press room before I could review. The composing foreman was a favorite of the publisher and got by with that little "sin" of shipping pages before approval. The reporter thought it would be changed during page make-up.

The publisher told me to fire the reporter. Reminded him the difficulty of finding reporters, and that I would not fire the man. He said if I would not do so, then he would fire me.

Immediately called Phil Swift and asked if I could drive to Napa. He wanted to know why, but I believed it was better to explain in person. He agreed and to Napa I went. After explaining, he asked if I could return and work for the publisher. Told him no. Couldn't see how that would work even though I liked the publisher and felt bad about the event.

While a truly nice fellow, he created a further problem with a poor decision.

With no managing editor jobs open in Scripps League at the time, Mr. Swift and Ross Game decided to add me to the staff in Napa until there was another editor's opening. Turned out to be a great career move. The stars were aligned once again, although because of a different reason.

Returning to Lake Tahoe that evening, I was greeted at my apartment by my three reporters. Mr. Swift's stepson, who had served as my sports editor before deciding to buy a weekly in Oregon, was also there to see what was decided on my trip. Informed them that I was fine, and would be moving to Napa.

My three reporters then showed me a letter of support. If I was leaving, the three reporters had a letter of resignation for the publisher. Mr. Swift's stepson had been my sports editor, and was training in the press room before moving to Oregon.

While I tried my best to talk them out of resigning, they had decided. The next morning, they gave the publisher the letter. The three reporters left and the publisher had to produce the newspaper until replacements were found. At the request of his father, Mr. Swift's stepson agreed to help the publisher produce the newspaper.

My staff felt my departure wrong just because I would not fire the reporter who produced the cutline and page. Even though they had families, they resigned and found other jobs. They quit over principle. Certainly admired them all for that since it has always been important to me.

The publisher was gone a few months later. Sometime afterward, Mr. Swift—because of my background at the Tribune—asked me to return to help out when the managing editor left. Spent a week helping produce the newspaper, then returned to Napa. The thoughtful Mr. Swift once again offered me funds for the week. Accepted the gesture, and he went down the street to his Napa bank, bringing back funds for me. An extremely thoughtful man, he had an unusual understanding of people.

Years later while attending a California Publishers Association meeting in San Diego, my former Tahoe publisher approached. He said he remembered a really talented, young editor from South Lake Tahoe. We shook hands. It was a gracious compliment. The past was history.

Neither of us mentioned leaving our jobs at South Lake Tahoe, and we had dinner at the same table. It was a wonderful visit. Except his wife did remember. She still had feelings because her husband was no longer publisher. Don't think she liked me very much. He then had his own public relations firm. An extremely fine man.

Next Stop, Napa

That chapter of my life was closed, and I was off to new adventures in Napa, joining the staff at the Napa Register. Working for managing editor Ross Game was always terrific. He was instrumental in my initial hiring with Scripps league, and he was totally supportive in Napa.

While doing some editing and producing pages, I also covered the City of Napa during a critical decisions era. The city council members were also sitting as the Housing Authority and Redevelopment Agency. Lots of meetings and many important decisions.

Napa City Council members also attended meetings in really nice places, like Hawaii. After some of the trips, the Register published an editorial outlining the expenses involved in such public-funded jaunts. At the next council meeting, I was sitting in the front row with my tape recorder.

All council members and the mayor took turns lambasting me for a detailed editorial on expenses. First and only time I ever received such attention from an entire city council. Their trips to several expensive places, to me, was a waste of taxpayer dollars.

Seems one council member attending would have been adequate. Monitoring such was the job of a newspaper. I did write the editorial, but it was appropriately placed on the editorial page.

Two and a half years were spent working with some outstanding journalists, and time really flew. It was a lot of fun living in one of the most desired areas in the country. Napa is in a beautiful valley with vineyards and wineries, only about 40 miles north of San Francisco. At that time it was possible to get around the city rather easily. More difficult today as people come from throughout the world to visit. Lots of traffic, both foot and automobiles.

During those years, my first wife and I had a daughter, Kathryn Elizabeth. They moved to Texas and we had an amicable divorce. Another important event occurred sometime later in Napa when I met a beautiful lady. She became my wife after my move to Utah. I will have a couple stories from my first job in Napa when discussing my return three years later.

Onto the Next Challenge

Mid-1970 brought a new challenge when Mr. Swift appointed me managing editor at the Logan, Utah Herald-Journal. It was only one of five daily newspapers in the state at the time, and he wanted new leadership for the editorial department. The newspaper needed to get local news up-to-date, and away from so many United Press International stories. It needed a local emphasis and he thought I was the person to get it done. He was right.

That was in June, and we agreed I would go there for three years, and provide strong news leadership. A truly wonderful man, J. Frampton (Fram) Collins was the publisher. He was totally supportive of my efforts, and was pleased the newspaper again became a leader in the community. Actually, the newspaper also played a small role in the state as well during my tenure.

Let me just say that the State of Utah has some of the most genuinely nice people I've met during my entire life. Certainly, Fram Collins and his wife Lucille were among those. Others included Gary Neeleman from United Press International and his wife Rose, Attorney General Vernon Romney, Governor Calvin Rampton, Logan Police Chief Eli Drakulich, Presbyterian minister Miner Bruner, and sports editor Kurt McGregor. There were also many others. Memories of those and others just warm my heart when the old mind travels back.

A large percentage of the population in Logan and Cache Valley were Latter-Day Saints (LDS). Still today I admire those folks, the way they raise their families and live their lives.

As managing editor, I still did a lot of reporting and covered emergency calls at night. Once again, friendships were forged with Police Chief Drakulich, and the Utah Highway Patrol lieutenant. The chief was a tall, large man and had been the chief for many years. He had a wonderful personality, admired by many. We became good friends.

Chief Drakulich was known by everyone. This was a benefit to me when we would attend a Utah State University dinner with several hundred people. USU was known for its great buffet dinners, and the tables were called by numbers. The chief and I always sat at the same table. Being police chief, his table was always called first. No waiting for the chief. Pays to know people in the right places. He was a peach of a guy.

Becoming friends and being a responsible journalist again enabled me to receive calls from the dispatcher when there were emergencies. Officers would have the dispatcher call me. However, there was one highway patrolman who offered a challenge. Numerous times people said that he would never ask the dispatcher to inform a reporter of accidents. To me, that was a challenge. Maybe he had a bad experience with a reporter in the past.

So, being the enterprising editor-reporter-photographer, I found where he had breakfast around 5 a.m. when he was on that shift. Popped myself out of bed, went to the restaurant one morning.

Went to his table and he invited me to sit down. After that, he would have the dispatcher call me on accidents. We were friends from that day forward. Just treat people with proper respect. And, report honestly and responsibly.

Not only that, we took his boat over the line into Idaho and fished for those fine, orange-meat trout. He had a farm in north Cache Valley. We hunted pheasant there together. We were friends as long as I was in Logan. Really, really nice man. Just had to show him that all reporters have a job to do and can be trusted. Thanks, Bob.

One friend made while in Utah was Gary Neeleman who worked out of the United Press International office in Salt Lake City. We met his lovely wife, Rose, and had dinner in Salt Lake City one evening. They are a great couple and have been married for more than 60 years. Our paths crossed years later when he visited me in Napa where I became managing editor. He was then working for the Los Angeles Times Syndicate.

Gary and Rose are the proud parents of seven children, and the family has excelled in life. Anyone who keeps up with news in this country will recognize their son David. He created Jet Blue Airlines. Other children have also done exceptionally well in life. Many who have visited will recognize the family-owned Zion Ponderosa Ranch in southern Utah. A daughter is in charge. Another son was founder of the nation's largest health savings account firm. He is also a Utah physician in charge of a hospital's trauma surgery. Another is a lawyer in Seattle. Others are entrepreneurs.

Gary, who is 85, is still very active, and he has 13 books to his credit. These are on Brazil where they spent many years. He was in charge of UPI's operations for South and Central America. Fluent in Portuguese, he still serves as Utah's honorary consul to Brazil. He has a fabulous history. They still operate Neeleman International Consulting in Salt Lake City.

Not being LDS, my wife and I joined a Logan private club where we could eat and dance to a band on the weekends while in Logan. Members would take their bottles of liquor, and it would be placed in a cabinet where it remained.

Members could then buy the mix and the bartender mixed the drinks from the member's bottle. It was the Del Mar Club, and they could sell beer, just not hard liquor. Had to purchase my rum from a state-owned liquor store. Must know what you wanted because all the liquor was on shelving behind the counters. Okay, Bacardi white rum, please.

Anyway, to show how well the police knew me, I was called to the phone while at the Del Mar Club one Friday around midnight. It was the dispatcher and a policeman wanted me alerted to an accident near the Utah State University campus. Hopped in the car. Off I went with my wife and my Preston, Idaho correspondent, Karen Stevenson. Four students died tragically in that accident.

That was the only accident for me to be subpoenaed to appear in court. When sworn in, the judge ask if I was the first news person on the scene. "I'm always first," I said, and that night was the only reporter/photographer at the scene. Testified to my photographs of the accident. Horrible crash, senseless tragedy.

There was one airplane crash that I vividly remember during my three years in Logan. An instructor and a student were aboard when it went nose first into the ground, plowing out a deep hole. It was gruesome, a jaw with its teeth left in the dirt. Think this was the first time I was aware pilots get vertigo, and they believed that was cause of the single engine crash.

Open Those Meetings

While not seeking investigative stories, my nose for news found them nonetheless. Certain actions would often peek my natural curiosity. That was the case before the mayor was sentenced to jail for four months.

I had written stories regarding spending and trip to Hawaii for the mayor and some city employees. This brought some unwanted attention to the mayor's office, and spending.

The county attorney filed a number of various charges against the mayor. He eventually resigned, and pled guilty to charges of making a profit out of public money, and failing to pay the city public funds he received. The hearing for his guilty plea was moved to Brigham City rather than Logan. While officials did not inform me, I did find out and there were some people surprised at seeing me in court. I had friends who knew, and they let me know. The mayor spent four months in county jail.

The Herald-Journal had published many stories and editorials concerning actions by the city commissioners. A number concerned lack of meeting notices, appointments by the mayor without a vote from other commissioners, and decisions behind closed doors. These actions caused me to write a number of editorials against such action, and a call for a new Utah open meeting law.

In a letter to Utah Attorney Vernon Romney, I sought his opinion on what action and discussions by public officials and their appointed bodies may take behind closed doors. The letter pointed out that local officials found it convenient to forget there was an open meetings law.

The editorial also noted that I had written Governor Calvin Rampton on a possible new law regarding meetings by public agencies. The governor responded to my letter, saying that "The press should never be excluded from a meeting that is concerned with public business unless there is a strong reason for doing this." A Salt Lake newspaper carried the story addressing the letter and Rampton's comments. United Press International also wrote a number of lengthy stories, citing my stories.

Gov. Rampton's response to me, and also quoted by other Utah media, stated: "You request that changes in the law be made concerning public meetings. I certainly would favor this, but would like to see your exact proposals before I would commit myself to a definite piece of legislation. Please let me know a little more in detail what you have in mind." He later referred it to the Legislative Council. While a bill made it through the House, it did not get through the Senate.

There was a great amount of publicity from state newspapers and media. Especially when the county attorney conducted his investigation, and the mayor was charged with several offenses. Certainly felt the newspaper had provided a great public service during those times. Personally, I did not need or seek the accompanying publicity, but it happened. Not running for public office, after-all.

Romney revealed that an investigation was under way into possible criminal activities by Logan City officials. At the time, he would not say if the possible criminal activities were linked to an investigation into handling of Logan financial matters. Romney did indicate they had something to do with closed meetings. Again, the Herald-Journal had numerous stories and editorials regarding those. Exposing problems, and keeping the public informed.

Attorney General Romney continued by saying, "If the investigation turns up criminal activities in connection with Mr. Shields' complaints formal charges will be filed." This was all taking place prior to the charges against the mayor. Romney's press conference in Salt Lake was in response to my letter to him asking specifically if advisory boards and planning commissions are included in the open meetings law. He responded by saying that "it is a misdemeanor for any public agency to take final action on public matters in executive sessions or closed meetings."

After leaving Logan, someone sent me a story indicating that two mayors had resigned due to improprieties in office. The story also indicated a former Logan City commissioner faced similar charges. Never received information regarding final status of those cases.

USU Investment Charges

While in Logan, I discovered Utah State University was buying stocks on the margin. There had been an order for that to cease. Met with a university official, and asked to review stock purchases. Oops, saw it was continuing and informed a vice president. That resulted in a Saturday regents meeting in Salt Lake. A story about the purchases was planned for the Sunday newspaper. The vice president knew I planned a story, thus the meeting.

My inquiry certainly got attention, and the problem was revealed in the Salt Lake meeting. The vice president called me after the quickly called regents meeting to let me know they had met. Guess he felt he owed me that much.

While the official divulged the purchases ahead of my story, it was laid out in the Sunday newspaper. This occurred not long before my agreed three years in Logan were complete.

After leaving the Herald-Journal and returning to California, someone mailed me copies of stories concerning a USU investment officer who was terminated. He was seeking a change of venue after being charged. The motion, which was denied, contended that familiarity with the case would prejudice jurors. The defense attorney also argued that a fair trial would also be difficult because of the environment. Other Logan officials had been indicted in other cases. Change of venue was denied.

Charges against the investment officer included falsifying investment reports, and making loans without proper authority. Stock investment losses were expected in the millions. I was also informed some stock brokers were charged. Again, I don't know the results of any of the charges since I had left the state. Logan was in my rearview mirror.

Looking back, it's interesting what a good local newspaper can do to help uncover such problems in a public institution. My following editorial indicated it did not mean the institutions are bad. Logan and Utah State University were both fine public entities. It is just necessary that proper oversight be given to operations and people. The amount of publicity given to public issues, and my look into the USU investment program played a part in these exposures. That's the role of a newspaper.

Those events just happened to occur on my watch as a managing editor. Often, the people involved are their own worst enemies by their actions.

Utah did not have a large population, but had two major newspapers in Salt Lake at the time. One was LDS owned. My reporting about investigative stories such as those above drew some attention from those newspapers, as well as Attorney General Romney. Early on after I had stories and editorials regarding the city, he called me one day and asked if we could have lunch in Logan. Well, yes, we could and we met at the famous Bluebird Cafe.

The attorney general and I became friends, and for some reason, he became a fan of mine. It was the only time in my career I could call a state attorney general and get through. He was always helpful, and would have an assistant provide answers to my questions if appropriate. When I notified him I would be leaving, he sent me a nice letter, calling me the best news person he'd known. Terrific fellow.

There was a radio talk show host in Salt Lake who appreciated my work. He would do on-air editorials in support for my reporting. My job was to report the news, not become the news, but it just happened.

One interesting moment occurred when interviewing Gunn McKay who was running for a seat in Congress. Borrowed the publisher's office and hauled in my typewriter to conduct the interview. It went about an hour and a half. Yeah, had lots of questions.

Mr. McKay sat right across from me in that small office, with my hands on the keyboard of that old standard Remington. We were eyeball-to-eyeball. Yes, my plastic eyeball included. I was still a very fast typist and kept popping questions while typing the answers, never looking at the keyboard. Pretty intense for Mr. McKay.

Mr. McKay was sweating on his forehead during the interview. When finished, Mr. McKay told me he certainly hoped I conducted an interview the same way with his opponent. He was an extremely nice gentleman and won the race.

While on politics, should also mention it was the first time to ever receive a gift from a governor, and the first time to be invited to a governor's home. Three-term Gov. Rampton invited some folks to his home one time during the Christmas season. It was an opportunity for getting to know the governor in a relaxed setting. A personable, down-to-earth, three-term Democratic governor.

Also, during one Christmas season, my wife called me at work. She said a Utah highway patrolman had just delivered a beautiful poinsettia plant to our home. It was from the governor. Thank you, governor, very thoughtful.

That's what happened during those years for a managing editor in a state with only five daily newspapers. Maybe recognition that our newspaper had some detailed stories reporting on a few governmental issues? Whatever the reason, those gestures from Gov. Rampton were unexpected surprises and appreciated. Oh, my publisher wasn't invited, nor did he receive a poinsettia plant. Help from Attorney General Vernon Romney was also appreciated.

A Story of Courage

It's extremely important to tell the courageous story of Herald-Journal sports editor James Curtis (Kurt) McGregor. Believe it was around the first of the year in 1972 when Kurt began experiencing breathing problems. He had been a good running back in high school, as I recall, and loved his job as sports editor. It was a pleasure having such a writer and sports fan in that position. Exceptionally fine young man.

Kurt's motor nerve health issues continued to escalate over a few months. Eventually, he began losing use of his hands. Probably around summer, his arms were also affected by the muscular disease which attacked his body.

Eventually, he could not drive, nor could he type his stories. Because of his devotion and desire to continue as sports editor, a young lady was hired. Kurt would cover various sports, and dictate them to a recorder. The young lady would type Kurt's stories so they could then be typeset for placement on a page. No computers at that time.

His courage was truly something to witness. He kept saying he wanted to continue to cover sports, including those at Utah State

University. If memory serves me correctly, during the USU football season, members of the team would sometimes carry him to the press box so he could cover the game.

As his health continued to deteriorate, Kurt's breathing became more difficult, along with losing most use of his arms and legs. In December, Kurt finally felt he could no longer do the job and he resigned. Reaching that point was heartbreaking for the many who knew his story, as well as for Kurt. Watching him struggling to breathe tore at my heartstrings.

To honor Kurt's absolutely phenomenal bravery, USU announced the Kurt McGregor Courage Award. With tears in my eyes, I watched as the announcement was made at a full 10,200 seat basketball game. Kurt was wheeled onto the floor to acknowledge. In halting words because of his disease, he thanked them for the honor. A touching ceremony.

Kurt became bed-ridden and I visited him at the home of his folks in January. Kurt knew his time on this earth was short. Never forget one of the last things he told me during the visit. "John," he said, "there is a big white desk waiting in Heaven for me to cover sports." He passed shortly afterwards. Keep writing my friend, you passed goal.

There are all types of courage we witness going through life. But, this was extremely personal for me with a front row seat to perhaps the most courageous person I've ever known. Everyone loved Kurt. He was also best man when Janice and I married in Logan.

Deer Was Laughing. But Got My Goose

Few more stories from Logan which my wife thought I should include. I'm not so sure, but here they are for your reading pleasure. Maybe a laugh if you have a sense of humor. May not get dinner if I don't include my deer hunting adventure.

The wifey still remembers my coat and snow boots right by the bedside, along with my camera, ready for emergency calls. That was so I could dress quickly and get to the scene of an accident or fire. She also mentions that we were disturbed by calls sometimes when she was trying to get pregnant. Read into that what you will. Maybe another laugh.

It also bothered her a tad when she had worked hard preparing a fine dinner. But, she understood covering emergencies was my job. God Bless her sweet, kind, generous heart.

One event she reminded me about during this writing was how the city snowplow dumped a large amount of snow in front of our driveway. Took me a lot of shoveling to clear enough to move my car. Our home was on a high hill overlooking the city. The beautiful LDS Temple and grounds were across the street, also with a fabulous view looking over the city and tall, vertical mountains west across the valley.

The hospital occupied the corner across the street on the other side, and another home on the fourth corner. We could see all ambulances coming to the hospital emergency room from the kitchen and dining room windows.

Of course there was no snow blocking the emergency room entrance, and none for the temple either, if memory is working. Don't remember about the home catty-cornered from us. The wife, to this day, believes our blocked driveway had something to do with my stories and editorials critical of the city officials. No way. That just couldn't be. Could it? Whatever, still had to shovel the snow to get our vehicles onto the street.

The following story is the one she insisted be included because she thinks it funny yet today. Never hunted deer while growing up in Texas. However, I went with my publisher, Fram Collins, and his sons one Saturday. Took a rifle borrowed from my photographer, Bob Trowbridge. Had never shot a 30-06, or whatever it was. We didn't see any deer that day, but there was a place where two mountains formed a very small valley. Surely, there would be deer along those mountains.

So, the following day I returned, taking my wife's 1968 Volkswagen, my pheasant hunting vehicle. For those who don't know, a shotgun is used for hunting pheasant. All you bird lovers and vegetarians don't get your shorts in a bunch.

Janice knows how to cook pheasant. Makes a great meal when cooked properly. Never shot them just to be shooting. She is a fantastic cook, and also bakes yummy pies and cakes. My favorite is egg custard pie. She makes a pie crust like no other. Certainly a lucky man.

There was about 15 inches of snow on the ground, and it was packed on the two-lane road to the mountains. Then walked back to the location previously spotted, took the rifle with a scope, crossed a shallow creek, and went between the two mountains. Surely there must be deer, and either sex could be taken. But, had never shot a 30-06. And, remember, it had a scope. Hey, I had shot .22 caliber rifles, but they don't kick when fired.

Got up the little valley, and looked up one of the tall mountains. Sure enough, there was a deer slowly creeping down to the valley. Waited until it passed through some brush, and had all the time in the world to line it up with the scope. Too long as it turned out. When it came through the brush, the scope was against my glasses. The deer was in sight. I pulled the trigger.

Boom.

Uh, oh!. My glasses split in half. Frame went into the snow, along with the two lens. Of course the lens for my plastic eye was just for show anyway. Plastic eye was still in the socket, thank goodness. Could have been lost in the snow. Found the frame, but not the lens. So, there I am with no glasses and a bloody forehead where the scope had hit. Yeah, forgot those guns kick when shot, but it was the first time ever for firing that large caliber rifle. No black and blue shoulder, though, since the rifle was tightly held.

With so much time to aim, surely must have hit the deer. Then climbed halfway up that tall mountain to the brush. Deer must be on the ground. More than enough time to sight with the scope. It had been a tough climb. Searched around, and in the bushes. No blood, no deer.

Bet that deer had a good laugh at the one-eyed hunter who couldn't even hit it using a scope. Doubt it even left any DNA.

Well, maybe it did scare the you-know-what out of that deer, but I wouldn't know. Didn't have my glasses for a proper search. Very disappointed while creeping back down the steep mountain. Nope, not having deer for a meal from this hunting adventure.

Always left my prescription sunglasses in the VW, so trudged through the snow, across the cold creek, and back to the car. Reached up to the visor to get the glasses. Oh no, they weren't there. Found out later the wifey had moved them to the other car. Bad timing—for me.

So, then drove down the snow-packed road and got to the top of a hill. Saw a car coming toward me and decided it wise to stop and let it go past. It stopped beside me. My friend, Sheriff Darius Carter, was the driver and asked what I was doing. Told him the story. He asked if one of the fellows in his car should drive me home. Thanked him, told him no, but suggested he not get in front of me. Actually, I could still see, just a little blurry. Damn the torpedoes, full speed ahead.

Well, the trip home went fine. That was my first time deer hunting—alone. It was also the last. And, it will remain so. Lesson: don't go deer hunting by thyself. For the beginner, they should put a sign on the rifle which says, "Kicks When Fired." Be advised, not like a BB gun.

Larger bullets—much larger.

While on my hunting adventures, my wife also reminded me of my first and only Canada goose outing. A friend, Jay, and others had leased around 5,000 acres adjacent to a game preserve near Brigham City. Barrels were placed in holes so hunters could not be seen by the geese in flight. That's where hunters would wait for the flock to fly over.

The day began early, and we were on the land after first light. Jay was driving his Jeep when I spotted a goose, just sitting not far from us. Pointed it out to Jay, and he stopped the Jeep. He said the goose looked as though it might be injured, instructing me to leave my shotgun, get out and run straight at the goose. According to him, the goose wouldn't run.

Well, he could not have been more wrong. While running at the goose in my hip waders, the goose also started running. Fast. Caught up with the goose just as it hit ice on a little frozen stream. Goose was sliding. When I stepped on the ice, it broke. Grabbed that goose by the neck. It went under water with my hand tightly wrapped around its neck.

My waders were filled with water, and my pants were soaked to the waist. Coldly walked back to the Jeep with my bird. Jay told me to wring its neck. Which I did. More than one way to get a goose for dinner.

Why is a mystery, but I had brought extra socks....thank goodness. Jay still needed to shoot his goose so he dropped me at one pit (barrel) and he went to another. He did not have wet clothes, so he didn't suffer as he waited for the flock to fly over. But I was freezing, and happy when it was time to go. Didn't care about shooting a goose with freezing hands. Already had mine.

Fortunately, Jay knew a lady who would pluck the goose for $1. Remember, it was the 1970s. A dollar was worth more back then. Jay gave instructions for cooking so it wouldn't be greasy. The wifey (a term of endearment) did a marvelous job of cooking that goose, and we had a fabulous meal. Like deer hunting, it was the first and last time. Only this time I took my own shotgun. Just not needed. Saved the bullet.

These hunting stories may leave readers feeling I'm not much of a hunter. Not true. My Dad taught me to hunt quail when I was nine, and pheasant came later. And, yes, I actually shot them from the air. Bang, bang. Maybe even bang, bang again. Quail or pheasant make a fine meal. Love fried quail, accompanied with mashed potatoes, milk gravy and biscuits.

Toward the end of my stay in Utah, I received a call from the Brigham Young University Communications Department. They invited me down and presented the Herald Journal a large plaque for our efforts in exposing problems. Extremely proud of that recognition for the newspaper. Smallest newspaper in the state, but we showed others how it was done.

Scripps League also owned the larger newspaper in Provo, location of BYU. Provo had one of the five dailies in the state at that time. They did not get a plaque. Don't recall any other newspaper being recognized that night either. Of course they were not exposing problems like the Herald Journal.

Should also mention while in Logan I received my first—and only—invitation to a presidential inauguration, this for Richard Nixon's second term. I didn't go. You kidding me, on an editor's salary at a small daily newspaper? Wouldn't have worked out anyway. Couldn't have afforded a proper suit or tuxedo on my salary. Besides, who would want to be around that many politicians at once? Even if they were Republicans. Make that either major party.

During my stay in Logan, the Herald Journal had become a newspaper recognized and respected for its coverage by many in the state. Emphasis had been placed on local coverage, as it should by all newspapers. It had up-to-the-day reporting, and adhered to strong journalistic reporting principles. Yes, the accomplishments made me a proud journalist.

The Herald Journal had met its responsibilities to the citizens of Logan and Cache Valley. That job provided me with some of the absolute highlights of my career as an editor, reporter and photographer. Left with my head held high, and Mr. Swift was pleased with how the newspaper had improved. Job accomplished.

California Here I Come—Again

Near the end of three years, Mr. Swift flew into Logan. He remembered our agreement that I would return to California after three years. We met for lunch, and he told me there was not another managing editor opening at a Scripps newspaper.

However, he offered to move another editor, and I could go to Petaluma. Or, I could return to Napa as assistant managing editor, and be the managing editor within a year. He said Phil Neiswanger—another wonderful person to cross my path—would soon be taking a job as publisher.

It was an easy decision. Became assistant M.E. and nine months later became Napa Register managing editor for the next four years. Phil Neiswanger was outstanding as managing editor and has always been a great friend. Wonderful personality and nice sense of humor (thank goodness for me). He was an extremely difficult man to replace. Recently spoke with him. God bless, he is 88 and lives near Portland, Oregon. During the call, we agreed it was great to work during the Glory Years for newspapers.

While it may be a bit vain on my part, like to think I'm at my best when there is a challenge. Becoming managing editor following my friend Phil was certainly that, and then some. During my four years as managing editor, we consistently won first and second place plaques from the California Newspaper Publishers Association (CNPA). It seems there were about 10 first place and six second place honors in numerous categories during those four years. The Register also won awards in other competitions, especially for promoting education.

Competition was extremely tough in our circulation category, probably with more dailies than any other circulation category, as I recall. Then, we won first for the most coveted category, General Excellence. My staff and I were beyond happy.

It was a first for the Napa Register. The Register also won first for Best Front Page. This not only recognized the coverage, but creative design. The look was pleasant, easy to read and contained photos and six to eight stories. Not like today's newspapers with only two or three stories, many not worth reading. Hey, a front page can still be appealing with more stories. If editors laying out the page understood design creativity. Not cookie-cutter pages.

Another cherished win was from the American Newspaper Publishers Association. An open category, it was for the Best Special Section. In the past, just like many newspapers of the time, we had an annual edition. Back then, they were often called Progress Edition, sometimes produced in slow advertising months the first of the year. They provided a service, and brought extra revenue.

Through the years these sections seemed very boring, so pitched a new idea to my publisher, Vin Brenner. This section generally had 96 pages, which meant four, 24-page sections. With press capacity, that would allow full color on the front page for the four sections. Today, everything is full color.

My idea was to call the section "People", featuring between 45 and 55 stories about "everyday" people throughout the Napa Valley. Six to eight photos accompanied stories of featured people, including youngsters, about their lives, hobbies or occupation. Definitely not politicians or people normally in the public eye. My publisher didn't think it would sell, and took a lot of convincing before he approved the idea.

The project was explained to reporters and editors. Their assignments were to begin finding interesting subjects. They did so, and came up with a terrific list.

Photographer Bob McKenzie was also an artist. He drew a wooden wine barrel, with a cork on top for each cover page. A large hole was then cut out for a single photo of one of our subjects. Each cover was a different color wine barrel enclosing the photo. The wine barrel was appropriate. Afterall, it was the great Napa Valley, known for fabulous wine.

About the only person widely known was Brother Timothy, cellar master at Christian Brothers Winery. He had a large corkscrew collection. We featured him on a cover, and it was simply magnificent. The section covers were beyond my expectations. Spent hours in the composing room having the photos trimmed tight, making them pop. It was not a technique used often at that time, but believed in that process and large photos. That later became popular in most newspapers.

A lot of creativity went into those pages, along with page one of our daily newspaper. Offset printing was still fairly new in those days, and the print quality was so much better than the old hot metal days. Like to believe our front pages were a tad revolutionary for the time, and they stood out. It was also a time when few were using full color on page one. Matter of fact, we had to send any full color photos to the Sacramento Union for the color separations.

The "People" section was produced and drew rave reviews. Superior Court Judge Thomas Konsgaard—a fine judge and person—called me. He thought it was the best section ever produced by the Napa Register. Very important, also, was a similar comment from publisher Vin Brenner. He thought it was great and rewarded me with a $50 bonus. While not much today, that and the thought meant the world to me. Vin was a good publisher and friend. We always worked well together.

It was terrific being recognized by the ANPA for winning first place nationally. Thought it was so great a large photo of the plaque was on page one to let readers know they were getting a superior product. This peer recognition with a national honor spoke volumes for the job we were doing as a newspaper. And for our readers.

A Changing World

My second tour of duty in Napa was in a changed world with the country out of Vietnam. Gerald Ford had assumed the presidency when Nixon resigned, and Ford ran unsuccessfully for a full term. The country then suffered through four years of the Jimmy Carter presidency.

There was a large media event in San Jose during Ford's campaign. He spoke, then asked for questions. Don't remember what it was about, but Ford said to me, "That is an excellent question." Okey, dokey, welcome to the Shields' world of journalism. Always tried to ask meaningful questions for a story.

Also got to see Gerald Ford hit a spectator with a golf ball during an Anheuser Busch PGA tournament at Silverado Country Club. A recent Register story noted that President Ford stayed in a condominium unit for sale. Wonder how much was added to the sales price because he stayed in that unit? Understand there is a plaque noting his stay in the unit. Whoopee! Add another $100,000 to that sales price. I stayed there once in a condo. There is no plaque noting my stay. Maybe they don't know.

Those also were years when Napa Valley was becoming one of the premium wine regions in the world, thanks to Robert Mondavi. Any serious wine drinker is likely familiar with his success after leaving the family-owned Krug winery. He built the Robert Mondavi Winery after having a disagreement with brother Peter. Krug was also a well-known wine.

Robert Mondavi's success turned out to be wonderful for the valley because of the worldwide recognition. During my first stint in Napa, seems the valley only had about 35 wineries. It's in the hundreds today.

Once was invited to a luncheon in a vineyard with some of the top winery owners during the late 1960s. Probably only about 25 attending. Their stories were interesting. And, they brought and shared their best wines. Trust me, I knew very little about wines, but certainly enjoyed the bounty that day. Sure beat heck out of Mogen David, the only wine I tasted before leaving Texas. My taste buds today appreciate a good glass of wine. Or two.

One of the advantages of working for newspapers was meeting some of the news makers, including some politicians. Just not all. First met Ronald Reagan when he and Paul Laxalt were governors of California and Nevada. They visited South Lake Tahoe and took the tram at Heavenly Valley. The press was sent up the mountain separately, of course. Both were personable men.

The Reverend Sun Myung Moon was also into a foray of the U.S. He's known for performing thousands of weddings at a time. Yes, it was also the day of the Moonies. Seems they wanted to have a place around or close to Lake Berryessa. Never happened.

One of the leaders would come into the Napa Register, sometimes with a beautiful cake. Accompanied by a female who looked a bit strange. Gave the cake to the staff, but did not try it myself. They seemed like nice people, but the movement just didn't seem to fit in the Napa Valley or Lake Berryessa. Or most places, really.

Another famous person to visit our newspaper was Tom Hayden, one of those arrested at a 1968 Democratic Convention protest. Well, he was also known as one of Jane Fonda's husbands. Or, was she known as Tom Hayden's wife? He was running for Senate.

Dear friend and publisher Bill Daniel called me to his office, and I was standing in his doorway, near a front counter. He informed me Hayden had called and wanted an interview. Could I assign a reporter? I had strong feelings about Hayden and his politics. Told Bill I didn't want to talk to the man, using an expletive which will not be repeated here. Would just have him interviewed by a reporter.

Out of the corner of my eye, noticed Hayden standing at the nearby counter, four feet away. More than likely he heard my comment. Nonetheless, pulled on my professional newspaper pants, introduced myself, greeting him warmly. Hayden asked if we could do the interview out front under a tree. Told him, "yes, we can sit under the tree." There was a little triangle with grass and it was one of those beautiful days in Napa.

We had a nice discussion, followed by a story, appropriate for any serious candidate running for the U.S. Senate. He lost the race. This was a prime example of not allowing personal feelings to interfere with being a responsible newspaper.

Unlike today's world of faltering newspapers, we were absolutely dedicated to keeping opinions on the editorial page. Today, there is so much blatant, biased reporting. Very, very sad. At least my career was during what most consider the Glory Years for newspapers.

Feeding Fish in the Pacific

Remember, newspaper reporters and editors are sought out by people seeking all sorts of publicity. A public relations manager for Hughes Air West called me one day. They would be making an inaugural flight to Cabo San Lucas, Mexico to kickoff service to what has since become a popular destination for the rich and famous.

The man asked if we had a travel writer or someone who would be interested in making the trip. Thought about it for five seconds, then told him, "yes, I can make the trip." And what a trip it was. The flight from Oakland had other writers from around the San Francisco Bay Area. Many were experienced travel writers. Some wrote for newspapers, others magazines.

They plied everyone with drinks, then we were off to pickup other writers in Phoenix. Drinks continued. Must be truthful, I didn't even try to keep up with the accomplished drinkers. Never have been much on booze. But, being no snob, a nice draft beer, glass of wine, or rum gimlet with Rose' lime juice are tasty. Not the squeezed lime, please, it just doesn't cut it.

Arriving in Cabo San Lucas, Mexico, we were bused to a Hyatt on a hill overlooking the water. There to greet the 16—maybe more—of us outside were bartenders and two seriously huge bowls of margaritas. Our group did travel writers proud in disposing of those. Hey, it was a warm, sunny afternoon. Besides, they were experienced at this sort of thing. So far, so good.

The group then proceeded inside to the bar where some experienced writer asked the public relations manager for his room number. He was going to charge everyone's drinks to Hughes Airwest. The PR man said he was not authorized to pay for all the drinks. After some discussion, the man gave up and told the bartender to place everything on his bill. Not sure if he kept his job after that trip. Probably assumed writers would have better stories if drinks were provided.

Guest speaker at the evening dinner was the state's governor at the time. He gave his speech, the group drank, and it was getting late. Now the PR man suggested everyone don bathing suits and we could sit in one of the three pools overlooking the water. Beautiful night and bright moon. Around 1 a.m., he ordered a cognac for everyone to finish the day, then off to our rooms. Some wobbled more than others, but it had been a fine day.

Earlier, the PR man asked how many would like to go ocean fishing the next day in the Pacific. Twelve eager, and some slightly inebriated writers, raised their hand, including me. The three boats were to leave at 7 a.m. Waking at around 5, I didn't feel so good but was determined. Just get up, get moving, enjoy the beautiful day.

After having a delicious breakfast buffet, I felt much better. Six of the 12 were present to make the fishing expedition. Other six likely overindulged the previous day. That being the case, it was decided to put three writers to a boat. The two boats made the turn around the southern tip of land, then into the Pacific.

It took only a short time in the high waves for me to feed the fish. First time on the ocean, and the boat was down in a swell looking up at the water. Still wonder to this day if it was the previous day's liquor, or if I just can't ride in a fishing boat on the ocean. We had two crew members on this pretty boat, but neither spoke English. Thank goodness one of the writers on our boat spoke Spanish.

After feeding the fish, drinking Coke and 7-Up were key to my survival. Also learned that fishing with an ocean line and rod are not the same as fishing for trout in Colorado. When it was my turn in the seat, a 30-pound Dolphin fish grabbed my hook. My natural reaction was to grab the line and reel. Uh, oh! It was a copper line and the burn scar remained on my left hand for years. Not supposed to grab a copper line in the ocean with your fingers. Those fish pull the line out really fast.

Despite the burn, I reeled the fish to the boat. Our guide pulled it up, then smacked it in the head with a large piece of wood, sort of like a baseball bat. Uh oh, again. He knocked the fish back into the water. In English, let him know if he did that to my fish again, he would be the bait. Not that he understood English, but he knew I was not happy losing the fish. My fellow Spanish-speaking writer would not relay my message. Likely afraid he would not get another beer.

Around noon we had caught several of the Dolphin fish, and our Spanish-speaking writer told the captain to head for shore. We were miles out and couldn't see the land. Upon returning, we saw one of the three writers on the other boat had caught a large sailfish. Doggone, wish that had been me.

The minute after setting foot on land, tossed down a couple Cokes and felt perfectly fine. Yeah, may not have been the previous day's booze, just the ocean. To prove that point, we had a marvelous Mexican buffet on the beach that evening. Glorious two days, and one of the benefits of working for a newspaper. Cabo is certainly a different place today, but there is no longer a Hughes Air West.

And, it was a legitimate news story with some neat photos for our weekend section. Cabo San Lucas became a popular destination of the rich and famous after airline service arrived. Still is today.

Cat House on the Napa River

If you've read this far, then you can likely surmise that humor plays an important role in my life. It's beyond me how people can wander through the years without humor, not being able to laugh. Especially at yourself.

That said, several funny events happened during my two stints at the Napa Register. During my first time, duties included visiting the California Highway Patrol (CHP) each morning checking accident reports. Editor Ross Game was known for hiring college journalism students during the summer. This was probably 1968, and he hired a long-haired hippy from back East.

My work attire included a dress shirt, tie, and usually a sports coat. Very professional. While grabbing my coat, this young intern came over. Ross had asked him to go with me to the CHP. Without hesitation, the young buck was informed he would not be going with me minus a tie, and wearing combat boots. Left him there a bit perplexed. But, he listened.

Next day, he came to work with a tie. He said the boots were the only shoes he owned. Okay, he could go with me, but he should use his first paycheck to buy some shoes. Lesson learned. Didn't matter to me that it was the day of the hippies. Don't know how that boy turned out in life. Maybe he eventually ran a large corporation. If so, just wonder what his dress code would have been for employees. It did become more relaxed over the years. Some businesses today are too casual. Not professional.

On Saturdays, the Register operated with a minimum editorial crew. One such morning, after putting the paper to bed, there was a humorous moment. A reporter, crawled from his desk and was squawking like a turkey. We were laughing as he made the sounds. Mr. Swift just happened to come into the department from his office around the corner. He had a smile, and just shook his head at the reporter making like a turkey taking flight. Those of us on duty cracked up.

Another time, a new, relatively naive, advertising salesman just happened to be in the office on a Saturday morning. Well, my sense of humor got the best of me. From the editorial department I called his phone extension, and he answered. With a disguised voice, I told him I was calling from the "Cat House" located outside of town on the Napa River and was interested in placing an advertisement.

The young man said he could help me, and wanted to know the type business of the "Cat House". I explained that we were an entertainment business, providing prostitution. I was watching as the red headed, pale skinned young fellow's face turned red and he began to stutter. I asked if he could take my information. As he gathered his thoughts, I wanted to know if he could still help me. Stuttering a bit, he said he would have to check with his boss on Monday, but didn't believe The Register accepted that type advertising.

At that point, I hollered at him, letting him know it was me, and he was off the hook. Yes, I am bad for practical jokes.

On another Saturday, I was in a humorous mood again. Phil Neiswanger is just a terrific fellow and was always courteous and considerate to everyone. Well, went to the front of the building and called his number. Told him I was getting married at a local pizza parlor that afternoon, and felt it was unusual enough to deserve a photographer and reporter. Again, used a disguised voice.

Watched as he walked to the photographer's schedule. He asked the wedding time, and began writing an assignment for a photographer. Phil then said he would have someone there for the wedding. Walked back and asked if he had received a call about a wedding at a pizza parlor. He said yes, and asked how I knew about the wedding. Okay, told him that was me on the phone and there was no wedding. He just smiled. He was accustomed to my unusual sense of humor.

Remember, these were different times in the world and employers were held to different standards. Same decisions would not be considered years later, especially today. Well, there was one reporter inherited when I became managing editor.

Let's just call the reporter Joe for purpose of this story. No reason to embarrass the poor fellow after all these years. After all, he may have become a huge success in life. Possibly in government work. Government seems to recruit people with potentially marketable skills.

Well, Joe had a Master's Degree. As managing editor, I was one of the few in editorial without a college degree of some type. One of my talents was a knack for remembering a reporter's skills, or lack thereof. In editing Joe's stories in different weeks, he had misspelled the same word twice. And, it was a fairly simple word.

After the second time, Joe was informed that if he misspelled the word a third time, I would get on his desk and remind him how to spell the word. Just tired of making the same correction. Teaching is part of an editor's job. That does not include constantly correcting a reporter—for the same mistake—who has few spelling skills. They need to find another line of work. No computer with spellcheck during those years.

In a later story, he misspelled the word a third time. Took the copy (no computers then), went over, hopped on the desk, and reminded him how to spell the word. Case solved. Couldn't do that today because I would likely get sued—and fired. Probably wasn't a great idea, even during those years. It seemed to be effective at the time. Further, it would be impossible for me to hop up on a desk today. Even if, getting off would be dangerous. Just too old.

Guess Joe was just one of those folks without spelling skills. Maybe he went into a field which did not require spelling. Guess it wasn't necessary for a master's degree. He also had a smart wife as I recall. Heck, might have received a master's degree had I remained in college. Nah, probably not. Too boring, and in a hurry to grab all the excitement which life offered. Besides, my spelling skills were learned in grade school.

Another reporter started his journalism career at the Napa Register. He returned to the city for a visit many years later. Michael Fitzgerald was that reporter, apparently traveling a lot, and writing a blog. The blog said: "A good portion of the war stories I tell have to do with that newspaper, and the wild man editor (John Shields) I worked for. I knew absolutely nothing about the business. I graduated with a degree in English, but got an advanced education in what a reporter needs to know—in about two weeks from Shields."

A former reporter sent me a copy of the blog. Michael's compliment gave me a warm, fuzzy feeling. Thanks Michael, and I consider your words a high compliment. Guess I was sort of wild at times through the years. But it was fun. Also like to think some wisdom and knowledge of newspapering were shared along the way.

Before moving along, it would be sort of criminal not to salute the most outstanding, gifted staff of editors and reporters during my almost 50 years in the business. They did amazing stories, with the Register recognized numerous times by peers in the business. Salute to all you fine folks.

Onward, Upward

As stated previously, the South Lake Tahoe Tribune and Napa Register were owned by Scripps League of Newspapers. The League owned about 45 newspapers throughout the country at the time, and had four primary owners. Phil Swift had acquired a nice interest as the group expanded over the years.

In 1975, the owners divided interest in the group, and went their separate ways. Edward Scripps kept the Napa Register and other newspapers. Mr. Swift then established headquarters for his group of newspapers in Carson City, Nevada. His newspapers were called Swift Newspapers.

Barry Scripps, son of Ed and Betty Scripps, was placed in charge of their newspapers. Once again, knowing key people at the top played a part in my future. We had become friends after his graduation from University of Arizona. He had worked as an advertising salesman at the Register, and we were on the same bowling team. Time or two Barry borrowed to pay the score-keeper. Always appreciated his friendship because he is a truly fine fellow and friend for about 50 years.

Those scorekeeper loans paid off because Barry gave me a $15,000 personal loan years later when he asked me to be publisher at one of the newspapers he oversaw. Just needed a few additional bucks until my home sold, and we could make the move. Keeping within the law, however, the loan was repaid with a small interest. That short-term loan was appreciated. Lot more than what I had loaned him for the scorekeeper.

While writing this, I managed to find Barry. We've kept up with phone calls over the years, but sometime ago his home phone where he lived no longer worked. Okay, so now I decided to track the fellow down using my investigative skills.

During the search a fellow by that name was discovered in a nice city. Hah, no phone number, but found an address. Sent Barry a letter and told him he could run but he can't hide.

A few days later a number popped up on my phone. Okay, probably another call wanting to give me a free ocean cruise. Or, maybe the one trying to give me a shoulder or knee brace. I'm getting older, and recently had a major back operation. Two, six-inch titanium rods and five screws were placed in my lower back. Titanium is expensive. They were recently removed—thank goodness. Also have a new knee which is marvelous. I will have the plastic eye shined and be a new bionic man.

Really could use a new shoulder. Not happening, though. What I don't need are more stupid calls offering braces. Just leave me alone. Or, maybe an NFL team owner could refer me to a massage spa. Or, maybe not. Don't need the publicity. Or attention from a spa. Or arrest by the police. Those who keep up with the news will understand why this is mentioned. Others, too bad. Come live in the real world by keeping up with the news.

Anyway, fellow at the other end asked if this was John Shields Investigations. Recognized his voice right off. Barry said he laughed very hard when he saw my letter and my opening line about not being able to run and hide. It was like old home week talking to this long-time friend. We first met in 1968.

Paid some dues for Scripps League and proved my worth over the years. The Napa Register was one of the League's largest newspaper after the split. Soon let Barry know of my interest in becoming a publisher. That led to my next opportunity. It also meant Barry would become another important person in my career advancement.

In May of 1978, he agreed to name me publisher of the Flat River, Missouri (now renamed Park Hills) Daily Journal. This is located about 70 miles southeast of St. Louis. Prior to leaving, my publisher and close friend, Bill Daniels, walked me through his method of tracking financials. He had a 16 columnar ledger to show every expense for every month of the year. That was to be part of the secret to my following success. Bill was another of my friends who has passed.

This allowed me to know where every dollar was spent. It was also before our smart computers today, and I never learned to use Excel. Enjoy math, just not being an accountant. That's for folks whose minds travel a different highway.

Barry and I each rented cars in St. Louis. He wanted to stop in Bonne Terre, just north of Flat River. Bonne Terre had been an old lead mining town, but was now in somewhat of a decline. Joined Barry in his car, and he drove through the town. It was far from impressive. Accepting this site unseen job was a mistake on my part, I told Barry. Seriously. Always positive, he then drove me to a nearby country club. Still not impressed.

Next day, however, he introduced me as the new publisher at the Daily Journal. A nice new building, and things were looking up. He left, then I went house hunting in nearby Farmington. Found a great home on one and a half acres. Fortunately, the first home we purchased after being married was in Napa. After five years—thanks to slow growth feelings—we more than doubled the purchase price. We could afford the home in Farmington. Two lots with beautiful, mature trees.

No Opossum Stew for Me

Turned out we had fantastic neighbors who are still friends today. One dear friend, Dr. Richard Winder, passed during my writing this little history. A sad part of getting older is the loss of good friends. Richard was one of those for over 40 years.

Another friend lived on the next street behind our home, across from our empty, rear lot. He was early to bed and early to rise. One night around 8:30, a resident opossum climbed the large hickory tree next to our second floor deck. The wifey left food for the numerous birds and squirrels. We lived outside the Farmington city limits. So, I opened the sliding door, and shot the opossum with my 12-gauge, about eight feet away. It fell to the ground.

Then my neighbor, Jerry Vivrett, hollered from his bedroom window. Could hear him because everything was quiet at night. "Did you git 'im, John," my friend asked. Well, the shotgun pellets hit that opossum okay, but their brain is very small.

After hitting the ground, that opossum quickly climbed another tree. So, I went down the stairs, then shot him again from the tree he had climbed. Made the mistake of getting right under him. That stinky, maggot-infested critter almost fell on me as he plummeted to the ground. That time he was dead. Dug a hole and buried him. Some would make opossum stew. Not me. Give me a steak every time. They are just a nasty, ugly animal. Don't know why they are on this earth. Can't see they serve a real purpose. Except for being a nuisance, and road kill.

Since I'm telling stories about my friend Jerry, might as well tell the practical jokes pulled on his wife Paula. The Vivretts were having a Christmas Eve party one night, and I was next door at a neighbor's home. Vivretts had recently booked an airplane trip.

Well, I called, Paula answered, and in a different voice I explained my airline company had made a mistake and undercharged. Therefore, we would be charging her credit card for our error. Unbeknownst to me, there had been an error and she said that had already been corrected. Well, I quickly explained that we still had not charged the correct fare, and we had already posted the additional amount.

We went back and forth for about five minutes, and she was going to call the credit card company. I explained it was Christmas Eve, they were closed, and it would remain on her account. So, I then went next door and she began telling me about some idiot who had called from New York about a mistake on her airline tickets. With the large gathering of friends, I explained it was me who had called. Everyone laughed. Paula promised she would get even. She tried.

So, on another evening neighbors were gathering to play poker. She had arranged with our friend the sheriff to have deputies come and arrest me for gambling. Well, it so happened I didn't attend. Paula has never gotten her revenge.

Another time all the neighbors were swimming at the Winder's large pool. My son came to me and said there was a large snake under our willow tree next door. Went over and it was about a three foot bull snake, not poisonous. I killed the snake, then went back to the swimming pool. Got in the pool where Paula was relaxing with her eyes closed on a floating device. So, I got in the pool and laid the dead snake across her stomach. She opened her eyes and it seemed her body went vertically two feet into the air. Everyone went into hysterics. Yes, we had some great times in that neighborhood.

Sorry for jumping ahead—again—but let's continue my story about moving to Missouri.

Just prior to going to Flat River, wife Janice had just blessed me with daughter Kristina. Our son, Philip, was five at the time and was born while in Logan. We only had to walk across the street to the emergency room for his birth. Kristina was delivered by cesarean and I watched her being delivered. After the delivery, the doctor turned and asked me if he could sew up the wife. Asked if he had tied her tubes. He said yes. Told him to sew her up. Kristina was a little beauty.

We now had our son and daughter. After 48 years of marriage, Janice is still fantastic and love of my life. Also a great mother, devout Christian and most giving person I've ever known. And, she's still beautiful.

Every January, publishers would go to Scripps League headquarters in San Mateo, California. As we were going through my proposed budget, one of the accountants thought he had found my numbers off by a large number. Flipped to my 16 columnar tablet. Nope, he was wrong, and apologized.

When we were finished, a vice president who supervised some of the newspapers paid me a high compliment after only seven months in the job. He was totally impressed with my budget preparation and knowledge. Thanks, Bob. On my way—again.

At that point I knew there would be other publisher jobs at larger newspapers in the future. After four years, and headed for the fifth, Barry Scripps announced a contest for the group's newspapers. There would be a monthly winner with a prize for the publisher showing the highest percentage net profit gain over previous year.

There would then be a winner showing the total highest net profit gain for five designated months. That publisher, his wife, and department heads and their wives would be sent on an all-expense paid trip to Honolulu, Hawaii for a week. Publisher and department heads would also receive $500 each. Clear the path, here we come. Loved competing from the time while delivering newspapers as a 10-year-old carrier.

The Daily Journal was finely-tuned and showing large net profit gains. It was poised for such a contest. A friend was publisher at the Hanford, California Sentinel. The Sentinel was also showing good gains. First month figures were announced, and we were first. Some of those beautiful red, flowers from Hawaii arrived at our home.

Fellow publishers still had high hopes, but the Daily Journal was first again the second month. Received a case of macadamia nuts. Same thing third month. That prize was sent to another publisher, although we were first again. Same fourth and fifth month.

The Daily Journal had won the trip to Hawaii. Must say it was fantastic. Must also say that we won by showing just under a 90% net profit gain over the five months for the previous year. Had that newspaper humming. I became known for making profits during my career at various positions with other companies.

Worthy of mention, we stayed at the Sheraton on Waikiki Beach and was at the swimming pool one morning. Noticed Merlin Olsen, a native of Logan, Utah, and former football star at Utah state University. Readers may also remember he was part of the great Los Angeles Ram line known as the Fearsome Foursome. He is also in the NFL Hall of Fame. Later, he was a fine NFL announcer, and actor in Little House on The Prairie with Michael Landon. We visited, and he nicely recalled some of his career. Pleasant and friendly fellow. He, too, is gone.

Beyond My Wildest Dreams

At this juncture, I must confess. A headhunter (recruiter) from Chicago had contacted me earlier in the year. While he wouldn't provide the name of the company at that time, it was a group of newspapers looking for someone with my background as a publisher, editor, and experience from the news side. Someone had provided my name. To this day the person who submitted my name for consideration remains unknown. Guess it will always be a mystery. Accused Barry Scripps of trying to get rid of me, but know it wasn't him. Barry, it wasn't you, was it? Been a long time so someone can 'fess up now. Promise not to give you the one-eye look. Many thanks to the person who gave my name to the recruiter. It was one of the events which changed the course of what became an exciting career.

The recruiter asked me to send information. He kept in touch over several months, and let me know when the list of candidates was narrowed to four. We also visited on the phone several times as he was sorting through for leading candidates.

The headhunter arranged a flight to New York City and a meeting with a headhunter/psychologist. I'd been to New York once before on a sales call. A real hustler, but nice fellow, saw me looking for a cab. He had a limousine, and I shared the fare with a pretty lady going near to my hotel in Manhattan. The limo owner then gave me his card to call when I needed to return to the airport. Later did so, and he picked me up.

Nice little man even offered to share his lunch. Who says New Yorkers aren't friendly?

Close to three hours were spent visiting with the headhunter/ psychologist. Guess he determined I was okay, with no serious flaws, because he later asked me to fly to Ithaca, N.Y. to meet with executives at Park Communications. First meeting was with Allen Meath, vice president in charge of the newspaper division. Also met separately with three other executives before going to lunch with Mr. Meath and Roy Park, owner of the privately held company.

'I Would Like His Job'

Will never forget the graciousness of Mr. Park, a gentleman from North Carolina. We met, then went to the parking lot, headed for lunch. He had a two-door, 1977 Lincoln Continental. He told Mr. Meath to drive. Opening the other door, my intention was to get in the rear seat.

Mr. Park quickly said, "no, no, you sit in the front so you can see the city." He would have it no other way, so I took the front seat and saw the city. He sat in the rear seat.

"What do you wish to do in the future," Mr. Park asked me before the car was started. To this day I still can't believe my answer. Well, maybe. Looking at my potential boss, Allen Meath, "I would like to have his job one day," was my comment. Talk about brazen and confidence. But it was the right answer for Mr. Park. Psychology 101. Or, maybe Psychology 202.

Just returned to Missouri, and Allen Meath called offering me the job supervising the Eastern Division of newspapers for Park Communications. It had five dailies, and some weeklies. They were located in New York, Indiana and Arkansas. Accepted the offer, but had asked for $2,500 more. The job was working out of the Ithaca headquarters. Gave my notice to Scripps League, even though my request for a higher salary at Park was rejected.

Still bothered by not getting the additional salary I felt was necessary to make the move, a few days later let Mr. Meath know I would not accept the job. However, in late April, Mr. Park and Mr. Meath were attending the ANPA annual meeting in New York. My decision not to accept the job continued to bother me. So, decided to send Mr. Meath a letter telling him I should have accepted the opportunity, and would not make the same mistake again. This letter was by design on my part. Always loved psychology.

(Remember, "Two Steps Ahead, Always" has been my motto for 50 years. Got to admit, though, as I have aged, two steps ahead is more difficult. May have to be satisfied with one and a half—or even one—step ahead. Keep a sense of humor, even on the way out. Hope the good Lord appreciates a sense of humor, or he may place me with some politicians. Surely haven't been that bad sailing through life.)

The day after returning from ANPA and seeing my letter, Mr. Meath called. He said to come on to Ithaca, they were giving me the other $2,500. Offer accepted—again—and had to tell my friend and boss, Barry Scripps, of my leaving Scripps League after 18 years. It was sad, but time to move on.

Working as a regional coordinator in charge of the Eastern Division was perhaps the most interesting and satisfying job of my career. Leaving short of three years, my division had grown to 11 dailies and probably 15 weeklies in five states. They were pleased with my performance, giving me additional responsibilities. Also did market analysis for some potential newspaper buys.

Park Communications went public during my tenure. What a wonderful experience working for a terrific entrepreneur such as Mr. Park. Mr. Meath was a consummate professional in his job. My knowledge grew by leaps and bounds during my time with the company, in charge of their largest division of newspapers.

Arrow to the Heart

It was a difficult decision to leave a job I loved, but the choice was made when returning after being gone all week visiting newspapers in my division. Son Philip informed me his school was having an evening activity the next week and asked if I could attend. Told him I would be traveling again. My 10-year-old looked up at me and said, "It's like I don't have a dad anymore."

Arrow went straight through my heart, and my decision was made to find a job with no travel. Supervising a division with newspapers in five states meant traveling about 80 per cent of the time. It was easy to understand my son's feelings about my absence.

While informing Allen Meath, he said I might not want to resign, letting me know he had accepted a job in California. He would be leaving in three months. He told me his position could probably be mine. But that job, if offered, would only mean more travel for me.

Mr. Park and others appreciated how I supervised my division. In charge of Park's largest division of newspapers, it was very possible Mr. Meath's position would be offered to me. It would have been supervising around 100 newspapers in a number of states.

When Mr. Park was told of my plans to leave in six weeks, he sent a nice letter from the sixth floor of the building he owned. He reminded me of my comment the day he interviewed me. That comment was that I would someday like to have Mr. Meath's job. He said he didn't want to see me leave, and later sent a second nice note down. Another vice president also did not want to see me leave, and was a supporter of mine.

Mr. Park was informed that my new job was in California, working for a family owned company with a daily and seven weeklies. He pointed out that he understood the father was a difficult person to work for. However, I would be working for the two daughters. But, Mr. Park was correct with his understanding of the father.

Mr. Park was one of the most interesting people and extremely successful. In the 1940s he was recruited to work for the Grange League Foundation and moved to Ithaca, N.Y. from North Carolina. The Grange apparently wanted him to find a way to sell their food products.

As the story goes, he knew Duncan Hines was a well-known food critic and travel writer. He felt using his name would help sell food products. Mr. Park got an appointment to visit Duncan Hines. In one story told to me, Mr. Park supposedly told Hines he could make him a millionaire. All he wanted was use of the name Duncan Hines. He asked him to think it over, and he would return in a couple weeks. He did.

Hines-Park Food was created, and Duncan Hines cake mix is still one of the most recognized brands today. Proctor and Gamble purchased the company five years later. Mr. Park then began purchasing radio and television stations, newspapers and billboard companies.

Park Communications later owned the maximum number of radio and television stations allowed by the FCC, along with the newspapers and a billboard company. Park Communications had over 140 publications, seven television stations and 21 radio stations at the time of his death. The company was later sold. Mr. Park had taken the company public while I was an employee.

Mr. Park would sit in on budget meetings and Allen Meath gave me good advice. He said if I did not know the answer to a question from Mr. Park, just tell him I would get back to him with the answer. He was 75, but sharp as a tack. While always following that philosophy, I made double certain that was the case with Mr. Park. Unlike others where there was an annual budget, Park newspapers did an update every six months. Mr. Park was nearly always present. His detailed knowledge of properties he owned was exceptional. Yes, the phrase "sharp as a tack" fit Mr. Park extremely well.

One of my work career traits was always to arrive at work by 7 a.m., if not before. Mr. Park would arrive around that time, or shortly thereafter. He led by example. Yep, he would usually see my little bright green 1971 Pinto in the parking lot when he arrived. Likely, that also made an impression. By the way, I loved my little Pinto. My wife and kids, not so much. They were overjoyed when it was later left behind in Ithaca.

That experience was fast-paced, working in corporate headquarters. Supervising newspapers in five states meant becoming very familiar with the U.S. Air hub in Pittsburgh. One very snowy night I had flown in from Waynesboro, Virginia. My small commuter plane was running late. After bouncing around in the wind and snowy weather, it landed at the opposite end of the terminal for my flight home to Ithaca.

While running through the airport, my briefcase flying, a man said: "Go, O.J., Go." Some will remember O.J. Simpson's Hertz commercial as he ran through an airport. That, of course, was before the murder of Nicole Simpson. Arriving at the airplane just as attendants were ready to close the door, I hurriedly took my seat. While late, managed to make it home safely on another cold Friday night.

Off the Road, to California—Again

At this point, it's important—as readers will later see—to explain how I came to Leave Park Communications, accepting the general manager's job for the group of newspapers in California. This company—first owned by the father and his wife—was owned by the three children. They inherited when their mother died. The father conducted board meetings. He rightly had a large ego, and was nice until you disagreed.

While still with Park Communications, a daughter contacted me about the position. She then invited me to California to meet with her, the other sister and the father. We had dinner on a Friday night, including the father's wife. It all went swimmingly.

Met with the daughters again on Saturday. They were explicitly clear that should they hire me, I would be working for them, not their father. Okay, that was perfectly clear to me. The company belonged to them and their brother. Their father had no financial interest. Important, and something to remember. They would make the decisions.

During my tenure, the father, in long letters to me, would make comments, and give instructions. Depending on the content, my response often was to remind him that I worked for his daughters, not him. Still have many communications and my response. Entertaining reading if I get bored.

The family was well-informed of my background, ability to supervise multiple newspapers, and for making a profit. Their company had not been doing as well profit-wise as they felt it should. They were concerned. Rightfully so. They understood I knew how to run newspapers—and have acceptable profits.

Upon my return to Ithaca, N.Y., the daughter who made original contact called. A salary double that at Park, plus a bonus tied to increase in profit, were part of my requirements to accept the job. One absolute was for a contract buy-out should they decide my services were no longer needed. It was a large payout, with no time limit. Or, if I was terminated for any reason. A student of history, that was my most important consideration for accepting the position. During the call, she informed me the termination portion was not acceptable.

Having some knowledge of the father and family history, this contract was extremely important to me, even though it was clear I would answer to the daughters. He had no hesitation in voicing his opinion. The son was an owner, but he did not participate in the operations. Spoke to him only a couple times, and he was always pleasant. It was understandable why he might choose not to participate in the operations.

When the daughter said they wouldn't meet my requirements, I thanked her for their time and flying me to California, wishing them the best of luck in the future. She informed her father, and it wasn't long until the phone rang again. It was the father.

The father stated he understood there was a problem. Explained there was no problem, but was informed they could not agree to my requirements to make the move. Probably near 80 at the time, he had a law degree and was an intelligent and highly successful businessman.

Rather than the large forever buyout, he proposed my larger buyout for the first three years. Then a reduced amount for years four and five. And, a smaller buyout any time after five years. He also agreed to the salary, plus a percentage of any profit increase. And, I would get a new Oldsmobile 98 as a company car.

Those terms were acceptable to me. The daughter, while not pleased with the terms, called shortly afterward and asked that I give my resignation to Park Communications that day. Informed her I would not do that until receiving written details of the agreement. Suggested she send me a Western Union telegram with the details. She sent the telegram as secretary for the company. This telegram became extremely important a little more than two years later. After receiving the telegram, I gave a six-week notice to Park Communications.

My family was excited about returning to California, out of the snow country, and having old dad off the road at home.

Everything went smoothly for a while. But, it was necessary to freeze wages until the operation turned the corner, making an acceptable profit. They were not overjoyed about that move, but it happened. Other steps were taken to improve financials. The company hit a record profit after my first year, then again the second year. Employees also got their salary increases returned after my first year. While not my favorite thing to do, freezing salaries set an operational tone and helped upright the listing ship.

The family hit a rough spot, however, and that placed me between the two daughters and the father. One daughter handled the newspaper's community relations. They decided she should leave her job for a time. This left me in a difficult position. One would ask me to relay a message to the other. It became extremely difficult and I did not want to be in the middle of family issues. Just wanted to manage the company, the reason I was hired.

The father would write me long letters with instructions. Remembering what the daughters had emphasized during my interview—that I would be working for them, not their father—I would inform him I did not work for him. Anyone who knew the man will tell you that did not go over well. However, boundaries were necessary because of my understanding from the daughters when interviewed.

At that point, I was tired of being in the middle of their turmoil. We had just turned our second record profit year. The company was running smoothly under my watch.

Board meetings were held at his company's headquarters in the Bay Area. The daughters and the son were not part of his newspaper company. During the February meeting, he began a rant aimed at me. As noted, I did not work for him and had decided I wanted out. Simply tired of being in the middle of their issues.

At one point, the father slammed his hand on the table, directing comments at me. I did likewise, told him they could not get along, that I had given them record profit years, and could do nothing to make them happy. By taking this stance, I knew where we were headed. This didn't worry me, knowing I had a contract, and would be able to find a job. Just wanted free of the turmoil. Felt it was certain they would fire me, and I would get my payout as outlined, and agreed to in a telegram and contract from the daughter who originally contacted me.

Sure enough, after my return home, the daughter from the Bay Area came for a visit, informing me they were letting me go. She said I could have an office in the building while pursuing another job. Reminded her of my contract, but she said they never signed it. Then reminded her of the telegram from her sister outlining terms of our agreement for the position. Her sister was their official representative when I agreed to accept the position. She didn't agree, indicating she was not aware of the telegram.

She wanted a copy of the telegram, and I told her at the appropriate time. Her sister had also given me a contract as secretary for their newspaper company. No way to know if she had seen the telegram, or contract from her sister. Didn't care. It would have been an easy victory in a California court.

Further, I made it clear that under California law, they would be subject to treble damages if my agreement was not honored. We came to an agreement on terms for my departure. Also kept the company car for a small amount. Paid that because I mistakenly thought it might have to be included as income. Oh well, small mistake on my part. Didn't say I am perfect, just good.

Once my job search began, it seemed certain that the father was talking to potential employers where I had applied. It was necessary to remind him he could get sued for such. That may have affected some job possibilities, but believe he stopped discussing me with others. It was just good to be away from that family.

For more than a year I sought work, but was still fine with the contract payout, and explored purchasing a 7/11, or a Johnny Quik. Two brothers had started Johnny Quik, and were building a new one near Modesto. Plunked down a substantial deposit, and was sent a large contract. My idea was to purchase several over five years, sell them, and go onto something else.

In reading the contract, it had a bothersome clause. One I could not accept. Visited the brothers in Fresno, and said it would be necessary for that clause to be removed. They said they had spent thousands of dollars for an attorney to write the contract and could not remove those paragraphs. They were extremely nice, bright fellows.

Asked for my deposit back, and that possible change of career became history. For the better, even though their convenience store/gas station seemed a fine business model.

Fate Raises Its Pretty Head

Then came a call from Bob Jelenic who was in charge of Ingersoll Newspapers in Princeton, N.J. Let me just say, Bob then—and later—became not only my boss and friend, but important to my career until my retirement February 9, 2007. Years after Bob first called me, the Journal Register purchased Ingersoll Newspapers and Bob became their CEO. It was a heartfelt loss for me when he died after I retired.

Bob wanted me to visit newspapers they owned east of Los Angeles where he was interested in me becoming publisher. He was not at all concerned about my issues with my former employer. After visiting the area, I phoned, telling him that area was not for me and my young family. It was too close to Los Angeles and I never wanted to live in that mess.

Bob then paid for me to visit the Ingersoll Headquarters in Princeton, N.J. First, however, there was to be a meeting with Ralph Ingersoll at a fancy hotel in New York City. At the last moment, Mr. Ingersoll decided to meet with me in Princeton. During the interview, he asked what I thought about being publisher at the California newspaper. Bob had also mentioned they had an opening at one of their larger newspapers in Anderson, Indiana, 30 miles outside Indianapolis.

Without hesitation, I told him the California newspaper was of no interest to me, and would much prefer Indiana. He said the decision was Bob's, but he would speak with him. Then met with Bob and some of the vice presidents. Afterward, he offered me the job in Indiana with a really nice salary, highest of my career. He always paid his publishers well, but also expected them to perform.

Will never forget, he gave me $25,000 and I would arrange my own move. For the time, that was a great benefit which was appreciated. He also allowed me to buy a nice, new reddish Oldsmobile 98 as a company car. Our son, Philip, also got a car out of that money. You're welcome, son.

So, off to Indiana we went, following a publisher who had been fired. Not only did I help resolve that, but successfully dealt with some union issues and prepared the annual budget. Should mention my office windows had bullet proof glass because of union difficulties years before.

After about eight months, Bob called and asked me to meet him at the local airport. The company had a neat little jet built in Israel for corporate travel. Had no clue about what Bob wanted to discuss until we met at the airport.

Not wasting any time, he told me the company was selling five of their most profitable newspapers, including the Anderson Herald-Bulletin. Reminded him I had not even been there a year, and asked "what about me?" He informed me they were selling to Thomson Newspapers, owner of the most newspapers in the U.S. at the time. With some, but limited knowledge, my feeling had always been that I would not want to work for Thomson.

Bob told me to work for them a couple months. Then, he said, if I wasn't happy he would find a spot for me at another Ingersoll newspaper.

After the sale, I was asked to update the budget for a meeting. Frank Miles, a nice man formerly in charge of all the U.S. Thomson properties, came for the meeting. He was helping with transitioning the newly purchased newspapers. He requested we have lunch in my conference room to discuss a revised budget. My beautiful and wonderful wife, Janice, helped win him over when she cooked cornbread, her tasty vegetable beef soup and a fresh-baked pie. Frank was overjoyed. After lunch, budget discussions moved along smoothly.

When we started the budget meeting that morning, Frank told me he didn't think much of some of my department heads. Quickly went on the offensive and let him know they did a fine job. That he was wrong. Simply, he said, "okay". To this day I believe he was testing me as a publisher with the comment. My response, I believe, gave him a positive impression that I could not be bullied. Think he thought that was a fine attribute for a publisher.

When we finished the budget process, he asked how long I had been the publisher. Eight months. Asked if I had received a raise. No. Then, he shocked me by giving me a large salary increase. He apparently thought I was okay because my impression of Thomson was that it was a company which tightened the financial screws. Maybe I was wrong, or maybe he was just impressed with me, my abilities, and background. Nice thought anyway, and a boost to the ego.

A couple months afterward, Bob Jelenic called, wanting to hire me as publisher for another newspaper. That was followed by two other offers. Told him I was happy in Anderson.

Barbecue Does the Trick

Then fate again intervened and Barry Scripps called in November, 1989 wanting to hire me as publisher for Santa Maria, California. He had me fly out for a visit. Driving down the several miles long main street, there was this great smell. Noticed a number of grills on wheels selling the famous Santa Maria Tri-Tip, a registered trademark. Nice way to hook this Texan, beef on a grill.

Santa Maria is in northern Santa Barbara County. An agricultural valley known for fantastic strawberries, Santa Maria is only eight miles from the Pacific. Cool breezes, mild climate, no air conditioning needed. Also no biting cold or snow. Frost on the windshield is rare.

After returning to Indiana, I accepted the Santa Maria job. With my wife and daughter, Bob Jelenic had recently flown us to Fall River, MA in the company airplane where Bob Jelenic wanted me as publisher of the Herald-News. It was tough telling Bob Jelenic of my decision about Santa Maria. He was very disappointed. Daughter Kristina, about 11 at the time, had been impressed to be flying in a private jet with plenty food and snacks onboard of that trip to headquarters in Trenton, N.J., then onto Fall River.

While in Santa Maria my job was working directly for Barry Scripps. As in all my other jobs, I was my own man, allowed to run the newspaper without interference. The vice presidents let me do my own thing, including making money for the company.

During my Santa Maria stay, got to meet one of my favorite comedians of all time—Jonathan Winters. He was speaking to about 900 at a gathering at the Santa Maria Hilton. When my wife and I arrived, he was sitting alone at a table in the large room. No one had arrived. We decided to go say hello. Couldn't just let him sit there by himself. That would have been rude.

Introduced myself as publisher of the Santa Maria Times, and he said, "sit down, sit down." His wife then came along, and we visited about 30 minutes. He cracked one joke and his wife said she had never heard him use it before. "That's because I just made it up," he answered. He was known for his off-the-cuff comedy. As opposed to so many comics today, comedy from Jonathan Winters was very funny, and clean. No bad language. Funny faces, funny voices. The faces he made were absolutely hilarious.

Let him know I was a record collector and had one of his albums in my car. "Go get it, and I'll sign it." When returning with the album, he said it was his first album, which I knew. The album is called "the wonderful world of jonathan winters." Yes, it supposed to be lower case. It has Jonathan Winters in the middle holding two masks, each showing a different pose.

On the cover he wrote: "To John—all three of us like you." He then signed it Jonathan Winters, 1998. It is one of my treasured keepsakes from all my years in newspapers. Along with the picture with Dolly Parton and my wife. It was a great 30 minutes spent with a marvelous entertainer.

There was also another event where he was the featured speaker. Another great opportunity to mingle with Mr. Winters.

A friend was in charge of that event, and he called wanting the Santa Maria Times to feature the event on a Thursday page for such announcements. Informed him it would cost for that to be featured on the cover section. He wanted to know what it would cost. Okay, that would be for me and my wife to sit at Jonathan Winters' table at dinner. No problem. We had the pleasure of sitting at his table during dinner. Some of my favorite memories.

Another famous face from the Santa Barbara area was actress Jane Russell. She also was a guest at a large gathering in Santa Maria. Etta Waterfield was working on the publicity for the event. She called me one day and asked if we might have anyone going to Santa Barbara who could drop by Jane Russell's to pick up a photo for the story promoting Jane's appearance at the event. Later called letting her know we had nobody going to Santa Barbara, 70 miles south.

Etta then said she would drive down and get the photo. I told her, sure, she just wanted to go to Jane's home. No, not really, she told me. Jane was her mother-in-law. Knock me over with a feather. I had known Etta for some time and had not made the Waterfield connection that Jane's first husband was former professional football player Bob Waterfield. Their son was married to Etta. Etta had also been Jane's assistant when she lived in Sedona, Arizona, as I recall.

The night of the event, I was standing in line to purchase a drink at the bar. A man tapped me on the shoulder and thought he knew me. Said I didn't recall meeting him, but it was possible. Let him know, however, that he sure looked like Waylon Jennings. He introduced himself, John Peoples, Jane's husband.

Peoples said he got told he looked like Waylon often when passing through airports. He further said he told Waylon that he just signed Waylon's name when asked for an autograph. Nice man, and we had a good chat while waiting for drinks.

Jane Russell later moved to Santa Maria after John Peoples' death. She also passed there. Just never know who you might meet in Santa Barbara County. It's home to many rich and famous. Older readers will recall Jane Russell being a famous World War II pinup.

Another well-known individual to cross my path in Santa Maria was Sonny Bono. Earlier generations will recognize him from the great Sonny & Cher. The famous singing duo was huge in the entertainment world. Many will remember their monster hit, "I Got You Babe". Cher is still performing.

Sonny was a congressman who was running for the U.S. Senate when he called wanting to visit in my office. He also brought his father-in-law on a late afternoon. While meeting a number of well-known people over the years, it was a pleasure to meet with Sonny. He was a truly personable fellow.

After some chit-chat, we got down to business so the reporter present could get a story. Then I asked Sonny if he was familiar with Lompoc, about 15 miles away. He said no, and I offered him some friendly, helpful advice. Informed him that Vandenberg Air Base was located there, and of its special economic importance to northern Santa Barbara County, Lompoc, Santa Maria, and the state. It is a site for launching satellites into orbit. Located right on the Pacific Coast. One of the most beautiful sites of my lifetime was an evening launch of the huge Titan IV during a sunset. While about 20 miles away, the ground rumbled as it flew into the sky over the Pacific and disappeared.

Felt bad for Sonny that day as he was very tired from campaigning, but did enjoy the visit. Nice and intelligent fellow. He didn't offer to sing a song. I didn't offer to have my picture taken with him. But should have done so. Just wasn't my thing.

Spent seven years in Santa Maria enjoying the area and people, until Scripps League was sold by Ed and Betty Scripps to Pulitzer. One day a Pulitzer vice president flew in on a private jet, supposedly to see how smaller newspapers operated. Pulitzer owned the large St. Louis Post-Dispatch. Not pleased at how the man looked around while touring the office.

Once he was gone, I called Barry Scripps and told him my suspicion that Pulitzer might be buying the Santa Maria Times. Barry knew nothing about it, but soon found out. The entire company was being sold. To Pulitzer.

Totally not impressed with Pulitzer's representative, later to be my supervisor. In late 1998, I called Bob Jelenic. He asked how I was doing, and then offered me a job—again—in Fall River, MA. This was the second time he had offered me this job. Since I was not happy with Pulitzer, accepted the offer. The salary was substantially more than I had ever been paid. That was nice, and it came with a company automobile.

Coast to Coast

By the time we left for Fall River, both Philip and Kristina were off doing their own thing in California. Just me and my wife, so off I went while she sold the house in Santa Maria. Looked for a home, but also placed an advertisement in the Fall River Herald-News. Found a condominium on the Taunton River. It is really a gorgeous bay, leading to the Atlantic.

From our condominium there was a beautiful water view, the light tower in the bay, and the large bridge leading to Providence, RI about 25 miles to the west. After purchasing the condo, an auction was being held for a condo in another building next door. Thought it was a great deal, so bought it, too. Sold it within a month, clearing about $25,000. Yep, Fall River was turning out okay.

The wife sold the home in Santa Maria and joined me for our first venture at living on the East Coast. There was a large Portuguese community of wonderful people. We discovered the great food in the Portuguese restaurants. Let me tell you, the servings were more than generous.

About 200 of the 220 Herald-Bulletin employees were unionized. One funny incident occurred when we were offsite for negotiations. The union rep from Boston was about 20 or so minutes late. Calling a department head, she informed me the pony-tailed union rep was in my parking lot talking to my employees.

When the rep did finally arrive, I reminded him of the meeting time and informed him if he was that late again, we would reschedule the meeting. He raised from his chair and told me sometimes he just wanted to punch me. "I'm here, knock yourself out," I told him. Red-faced, he took his seat. Don't push a Texan. Believe if I had complained, I could have prevented him from ever doing negotiations at that newspaper again.

Guess this is a good place to mention that during our move from Santa Maria we had to store all our shipment for about six weeks, waiting for the condo to be vacated. When it arrived and we checked off the boxes, 20 were missing. Contacted the moving company supervisor and he said they were missing when the truck was unloaded. That would seem to mean the driver took our boxes. So, why did they not let me know about the missing boxes when they arrived? Might have been able to track them. Couldn't six weeks later.

For years I had attended garage and estate sales collecting records. A moving box would hold 100-110 records, meaning the shipment was missing about 2,000 33s. They were gone, and the moving company had no clue where they were. The company offered to pay me 60 cents a pound, and later $1 a record. Told them many were very valuable, and that I had purchased replacement value insurance.

The moving company and I tussled, and I eventually hired an attorney. Knew the main attorney, but he assigned me someone not with the firm very long. She filed a case with the U.S. Federal Court in Boston since it was an interstate claim. Eventually, we had a pre-trial with the federal judge in charge.

In an earlier hearing, she said the judge told the moving company that a relative was a collector and would be upset if that happened to him. My claim was for $50,000, but unbeknownst to them I did not have a list of the records. Prior to the move my collection was about 8,000, and I disposed of around 5,000. Still have 1,000 today. Fortunately, these were in the house and not marked as records. Thankfully, these boxes contained records from some of my favorite artists such as Elvis, Merle Haggard and Frank Sinatra.

Prior to the pre-trial hearing the moving company offered $9,000, but I told them it would take $15,000 to settle. They wouldn't budge. During the hearing, the judge asked about settlement talks and the moving company's Harvard-educated attorney finally said they would go to $11,000. My attorney was doing the talking, but felt the message wasn't being presented as I wished. The judge then allowed me to make the presentation.

The judge asked what amount it would take for me to settle. Again, that day, I said $15,000. The moving attorney showed a little anger and said they would not give that amount. Suggested to the judge that we just go to trial, and I would seek the $50,000.

The judge flipped to his calendar, and said the trial could be the following Monday. "That's fine with me your honor," I responded. Opposing attorney balked at the quick date, so the judge then said he would hold the trial a week from that date. Again, the moving attorney balked, and the judge told him that he should consult with his client. Judge said the man could use his office to do so.

We had been outside the courtroom for an hour when the moving company attorney returned. Said they would just have to pay the $15,000. Told him that wasn't true, we could go to trial. He said no, they would pay within a week. Explained to him that he could handle right then, just write the check. Not a happy person, he said I knew he couldn't do that. Got their check within a week. Through my career the numerous tussles with attorneys always provided me with a little mind-game fun.

Here We Go Again

Less than a year in Fall River, Bob Jelenic called me and was moving me to CEO/Publisher at the New Haven (Connecticut) Register. With 100,000 circulation, this was the Journal Register's number one newspaper. It also had about 25 weeklies and twice weeklies along the shoreline, across from Long Island. The operation had about 1,000 employees. It also included a printing facility near New Haven which printed about 100 publications a week. The Register had its own press room.

New Haven is also home to Yale University. Oh my, a conservative CEO/Publisher in charge of a major newspaper in a liberal city. It was a big job, and the newspaper was certainly a player in the community. It also played a large role in the Journal Register's bottom line.

Bob sent me there because of my history at producing nice profit lines as a publisher. That didn't change in New Haven. There were, of course, other reasons for my success. Like to think my ability to manage and get along with employees was part of the reason for success. When there were unions, my ability to negotiate was also helpful. The Register had no unions.

With the wife selling the home in Fall River, I began looking for another condominium. My office—largest and nicest of my career—offered a view of the ships coming in from Long Island Sound. Should also mention it was my only office with a shower and a small kitchen. Could have slept on one of the several couches in the office and been quite comfortable. Probably should have, often spending 10-12 hours a day in the building. Weekends also took some time.

When looking out my windows one day, noticed what appeared to be condos across the water. At the top of a hill. It seemed they must have a great view of Long Island. Those buildings were just calling to me from my office and I went searching for the road leading to them. Located the condos and the view was absolutely spectacular. A man was washing his car at a condo providing the best view of all the units. When I asked if he knew of any owners wanting to sell, he said they had thought about it. Next day I called and he invited me to walk through his unit.

It was a townhouse end unit with a deck overlooking Long Island Sound. Two ships were crossing downriver toward New York City, about 90 miles away. He informed me they were the ferry boats from Bridgeport (30 miles) to Long Island. What a view. He said a neighbor with a telescope had watched his son docking in New York City. Talk about spectacular, especially with runway lights at night from the airport below. That did it, I had to buy this place.

Immediately made an offer, and the man accepted. He asked when we wanted to close the sale and I said two weeks. He gasped but agreed. Sure enough, we closed in two weeks, and he placed his belongings in storage. Never be bashful when someone wants to deal. Remember, cash is king, but I financed that particular purchase.

The Register was the second largest newspaper in Connecticut, and as such received a lot of attention. It also donated to PBS in the state. My wife and I were invited to a dinner at the governor's residence in Hartford one evening. Only 16 people were in attendance. They were large donors to PBS. Let me tell you, here was the Texas boy sitting with some mighty high rollers because of my job, and my company's affiliation with PBS.

When it came time for dinner to be served, seated next to me was Sheryl Leach. Don't know her? I didn't either, but found out she brought Barney to all the kids in the world. What a pleasure it was to sit next to this pretty, fellow Texan at dinner.

Discovered that Barney was created when her child, a boy I believe, was young and there was nothing on television for him to enjoy. So, Barney was born. Her son apparently liked dinosaurs. That's my recollection. Sheryl, please forgive me if that's not exactly right.

When it was time to leave, another donor was talking with Sheryl. She had driven from where she lived down I-95. He had flown to Hartford in his helicopter. Believe she accepted an offer to fly home in the helicopter rather than make the drive. Money and position have their rewards.

Should mention that the gentleman with the helicopter also invited me to visit. He had a trout stream of which he was very proud. Unfortunately, I never took him up on the offer. Should have found the time, since the stream was several miles long, and had large trout. One of my regrets since I enjoy eating and fishing for trout. Oh, well.

As noted previously, my boss Bob Jelenic was also a terrific friend to me through almost 20 years, but we would have our moments.

He was tough, but usually fair to those who worked for him. He always showed his appreciation for my abilities. He also used my negotiating skills with unions in newspapers, even though I might not be the publisher. These skills came from working in real life, not the classroom. Must say, it was fun and always interesting.

Never belonged to a union, although my dad did while working for Phillips 66. While not opposed to them, some demands were outrageous. Their reps from union headquarters often did more harm than good for the employees. Some of their demands helped drive change in the newspaper industry for employees when technology came along.

Importantly, I recognized the right of employees to belong to a union and worked well with most unions and reps during my career. However, if being tough became necessary, it was not a problem. While negotiating is serious and challenging, it is rewarding when all leave the table satisfied.

Interestingly, one union representative and I became friends. He would tell me what the employees wanted. I would then tell him what my company was willing to give. We would sometimes come to an understanding. We would have a meeting, and he would present their demands, but we understood where the negotiations were headed. He did his job, and I did mine.

One of the benefits in New Haven was an absolutely fantastic assistant. She was a sweet, classy lady named Ann Marie Brennan. Extremely competent and professional. Every CEO should be so fortunate. My office was located on the second floor. When we spoke recently, she told me I had to include one story. So I will.

My CFO's office was at the other end of a very long hallway. It took time to get there, so I would usually run to his office. Ann Marie said a person below on the first floor called her one day to find out about a loud noise. Well, it was me running down that long hall to the other end. Employees came to recognize my sprinting to the CFO's office. Hey, time is valuable. Always wore a tie-tack, so the tie would fly up, but remained in place. Maybe I should have run track while in high school

I thought we were doing well in New Haven, but Journal Register was a public company and Bob Jelenic was always under a lot of pressure for JRC to produce as a company. To this day I believe that may have led him to move me from New Haven after a little over two years. While not divulging how much The Register, affiliated newspapers and printing operation made, they were certainly profitable. The profit percentage had to be some of the best among newspapers. Some newspapers had their challenges. When a public company, the bottom line includes all operations, and is an important number for investors.

Last Career Change

Regardless, Bob told me he would be making a change. Didn't give me a reason, but I could guess. He said the only property which needed a publisher was Taunton, MA. I was floored because of our profit line. To say I was not happy would be an understatement. He told me the salary—a reduction —and I told him I would not accept it. He boosted it substantially. Okay, while extremely peeved, believing it was an unfair move, the offer was accepted. Seemed unfair, but he had a job to do and had his reasons.

Bob also told me to take the company Lincoln Continental purchased upon arrival. That was also a nice gesture. When I first arrived in New Haven, he told me to go buy a new car. Informed him I would like a Toyota Avalon. That didn't fly because he said it had to be American-made, therefore the Lincoln. Bought my own Avalon after retiring, and still love that car. Also enjoyed the Lincoln Continental.

Bob had a vice president in charge of the New England properties. He told me I would be working for that man as we sat in the Taunton Gazette parking lot prior to introducing me as the new publisher. Simply told him I would not work for the man. Didn't like him. So, Bob then said I could report directly to him. That was fine with me.

An interesting incident did occur after my move, and the company had a meeting for publishers, vice presidents, board of directors, and financial people. It illustrates, I believe, how strongly Bob felt about my abilities. Just before lunch, he was making a speech, and made a mistake, forgetting my feelings about being moved from New Haven. While talking on a subject, he said, "John, you remember in New Haven," referring to my time there. Couldn't believe he would even mention me regarding anything about New Haven. It was in my rearview mirror. He knew I didn't believe my move was just.

My response before he could finish on the topic was to stand up, and said, "Bob you don't want to go there." I immediately walked out of the room with all those publishers, and members of the board of directors. Publishers told me Bob, obviously a little stunned at my departure, took a minute, maybe two, to collect his thoughts and then said it was time to break for lunch.

Several publishers approached me in the hall, and said I was their hero. No one, but no one, would have ever dared walk out on Bob as I had just done. Or, maybe no longer be employed. Well, we went back to the meeting and Bob never mentioned the incident. He did invite me and three or four other publishers for a special after dinner drink which cost about $25 a person—per drink. But, Bob and I always had a great relationship, not only as boss and employee, but as friends. Perhaps he realized he made a mistake. And he did.

While not overjoyed about the Taunton move, I took it in stride. As it turned out, it was a great move which got me to retirement. The Gazette had wonderful employees. Bill White was the controller. I had two other fantastic department heads in other newspapers through the years, but Bill was the very best.

He did a fantastic job, and made my last seven years in the business easy. There is nothing he can't do, nor any job he can't handle. He gives new meaning to the term multi-talented. Thanks Bill, you were No. 1. And, that's out of a few thousand. Special guy, special friend.

One very sad event occurred after the move to Taunton. It was September 11, 2001 when two Boeing 767s destroyed the World Trade Center Twin Towers in New York City. Almost 3,000 people died, and both of the tourist-attracting towers collapsed. This terrorist attack forever changed this country then and for the future.

It was in Taunton that we decided to venture into Thoroughbred horse racing. We bought a horse and a half (yeah you can do that). They say horse racing is for the rich. They're right, I'm not rich, and should not have been such a fool. But it was fun. Anyway, we had a horse from the Seattle Slew and Storm Cat lines, so assumed that was good.

We had our mare bred to a stud from the Storm Cat line. Named the filly Stormy's Lightning, but found out it was expensive to train in Kentucky. She was born in Lexington, but moved her to Texas for training and racing in a three-state area. She won four races, and finished in the top three 40 per cent of the time in 20 races if memory is working. Unfortunately, they were not big money races. It was fun and, of course, was a business expense. Heed the advice, don't have a race horse unless you have big bucks, or can do the training yourself.

'I Came to Learn You People'

Senator Ted Kennedy stopped by to visit while campaigning in Taunton. In 2006, he was in his last run for Senate and came by with three people. One was his former Harvard roommate. Fellow was a Texan. Imagine them getting past the language barrier of a Bostonian and a Texan. At least both could then claim to know at least two languages.

During the visit, Sen. Kennedy reminded me I was also a Texan and asked why I moved to Massachusetts. "Senator Kennedy, I came to learn you people." That drew a round of laughter. Afterward, I was talking with his college roommate in the lobby while Ted visited with my employees. The roommate was telling me stories about their time at Harvard. Ted told me he would return again to hear about those stories. It didn't happen. He was reelected, and I retired.

During that visit I told my managing editor and reporter that I wanted to have a conversation with the senator the first 30 minutes, and not to interrupt. They didn't. One of my first questions was to ask how could Congress make major changes in Social Security. It happened when he was a young senator. Will never forget him saying it was one of the worst travesties to come out of Washington, D.C.

It was, still is today, and will continue to be so in the future. Shame on Congress. That money belongs to workers. It was paid for by the employees and their employers. Not for the expansion to some who could access the funds with changes in the 1960s. It is not an entitlement as claimed by many. The funds have not been managed properly. Social Security could have been more secure without the changes enabling access by those not in the original program. Mismanagement of those funds has forever damaged that program.

Senator Kennedy was known for many things other than Chappaquiddick. One was his attention to detail, and notes to those he met or communicated with through the years. When I was publisher in Fall River, he wanted the newspaper to co-sponsor an economic forum at the local community college. We did.

After Sen. Kennedy returned to Washington, a phone call came from Joseph Kennedy's office. He led an organization which provided fuel assistance to the needy. His aide asked if I would hold for Joe Kennedy. Then he said he had to hang up, that Joe was calling for him. Well, okay, I wasn't that important, it seemed. That was just before noon.

After returning from lunch, my phone rang and assumed it was Joe Kennedy's office again. There was this deep voice at the other end. "Hello, John, this is Ted Kennedy. I just wanted to call and thank you for helping with the forum yesterday." Again, attention to detail. Believe the call may have come from the Senate floor during the Clinton impeachment hearings.

While disagreeing with Senator Kennedy philosophically, give him credit for representing his like-minded constituents.

Should also mention that I am probably among the few to turn down a dinner invitation to Sen. Kennedy's home at the Kennedy Compound in Cape Cod. Received a call from someone in his Washington office one day. The person said Sen. Kennedy would like for me to attend a dinner at his home on the Cape. Asked if my wife was invited, and she said, "no, sorry." Told her to let the senator I would not be attending.

A few days later, someone higher up the food chain at his Washington office called. He said the senator would really like for me to attend the dinner. "Is my wife invited," I asked. He apologized profusely, but said no. Told him to inform the senator I would not be attending. It was likely a gathering including journalists since he was running for reelection. Didn't care, it was a Friday night. My wife still feels special since the invitation was not accepted because she was not invited.

Missed my chance to meet some mucky-mucks, drink fine booze, and eat fine food, I'm sure. But, guess what, I don't care. Makes a better story this way. At least it seems so to me. But, Ted was always nice to me. And, Joe Kennedy never called back. His loss because I'm a great conversationalist, even with my conservative leanings. Have no idea why he wanted to speak with me anyway. Obviously wasn't that important, so just as well we did not connect.

So, having finished seven pleasant years as publisher in Taunton it was time to get ready for retirement. We had visited Phoenix a couple times and thought it would be a great place to spend the remainder of our days. Sunshine year 'round. I had moved 11 times since leaving Texas in 1965, and we lived in places where it was cold and had a lot of snow. We wanted to live where it had no snow, but where it could be seen on distant mountains. That's what Arizona offered.

We bought a home in Arizona while still living in Massachusetts. Our daughter in San Diego had a traveling job and could live anywhere, so she moved into the new house. My wife joined her several months later, and I gave Bob Jelenic my notice. Bob said I couldn't retire then because Journal Register was selling its New England properties, including Taunton. He needed my help until the sale was finalized.

Bob made me an offer which was difficult to refuse. It meant money for me when the sale was final. But, only if the new owner put me on the termination list. He said since I was selling our condominium in Taunton and my wife was moving to Arizona, the company would pay for an apartment until the deal closed.

Well, the new owners wanted me to remain as publisher. Simply said I didn't want to work for them, retirement was calling. Finally, not long before the sale finalized, they agreed to place me on the termination list. Hooray, hooray! At last, I could retire to the sunshine. I was 64 years old.

Onto Retirement

Day after the close, hopped a plane out of Providence, R.I. to Phoenix, February 10, 2007. My wife was concerned I would become bored after working 10-12 hour days, including many weekends along the way. She was wrong, I've enjoyed 12 years of retirement, and am a familiar face at our county library a half mile from the house. Also, I attend a neighborhood gathering most mornings. So, no, I'm not bored.

Today, anywhere from three to seven or eight of us gather at one of our homes each day for 7 a.m. coffee. And, usually, dough-nuts or other desserts. Need sugar along with the coffee. While we really are friends, we label each as an associate. We discuss ways to solve the world problems. Arguments are lively since it's about an even split between Republicans and Democrats. Being the author here, I get to list Republicans first. No one with thin skin allowed.

Topics and insults get brutal at times. Just a way to sharpen our senses, and get the day off to a quick start. Too much caffeine will do that to a person. As a defense for the two to four cups each, they point to a medical study showing it is good for the body. It's justification, and they leave wired after two hours. A little about each coffee "associate" follows:

One from New Jersey is widely-traveled, just not in the middle part of our great country. He once had a stopover in Texas, but was not impressed. My suspicion is that because of his accent they wouldn't let him leave his gate area. Maybe they won't let him have a pass to get through the state again. Should have shown his fireman's badge. His recall of events, dates, and names is remarkable. Only thing, we can't challenge his recollections for fact because we weren't present. When his day to provide coffee, it's with an old percolator, not a Mr. Coffee. Sometimes it's necessary to have a knife to slice his dark offering. Makes his coffee black and strong. So strong, the cup could likely walk on its own.

The second coffee member from New Jersey made a few appearances in my stories. He, too, was a fireman, but now he looks like an Arizonan. He's the tallest in our group, and a student of history. He is proud of his 1958 red and black Rambler, and a Dodge pickup truck he's had for years. Previously had a 1968 Ford Thunderbird, but sold after buying a 1977 Ford Thunderbird similar to one owned years ago. His wife likes the newer red and white better. Keeps the vehicles shining, and helps companies selling car wax remain in business. He's owned horses, but sold his last horse named Coffee, and may never ride again. Like the rest of us, he's getting older. Bones tend to become brittle. Falling from a horse would be bad.

Yet another coffee attendee is from around Cleveland, and has a funny accent. Almost have to be bilingual—or more—to understand the different dialects in our group. A car enthusiast, he has a 1966 Ford Mustang fastback in desperate need of renovation. Cops would have it towed to a junkyard if found beside a road. Like many older folks, he owns a red Corvette. Fortunately, he lives about a mile and a half from our development. He's a retiree from Snap-on, the tool maker.

One coffee mate is an accountant from Illinois and is limited (we try) to 11 words per gathering. Unfortunately, he learned the hard way to hire a fellow to trim his palm trees. That was after trying himself. He was rewarded with scratched, bloody arms. Maybe he learned his lesson. Besides, tree trimmers need the work. He has a push lawn mower which is likely a collectible, but he wants $40 for it. My tall New Jersey friend keeps offering to buy for $20, but he won't sell. Don't know why since he has fake grass. Perhaps he should contact Antiques Roadshow about the lawn mower.

Another in our group was a crane operator. His toys include a Corvette, Jeep and a motorcycle. Seems only old guys own Corvettes. Sort of ridiculous. It is funny to watch them struggle to get in and out of the vehicle. He and the tall, former fireman have pacemakers. Just don't know how long their batteries will last. Better hope they are not those which explode. And, if they are the 7-year batteries? Oh well. Been fun.

Then there's one who wears boots, western shirts, and owns a horse. A native of Indiana, he's kind of a normal fellow. Normal because he leans conservative. He owns a beautiful 1948 Chevrolet with a V8, and power windows and seats. Those are not original. It can be purchased for $25,000. A Post Office retiree adds more flavor to the coffee group. Wouldn't advise breaking into his home. He has guns and lots of ammo.

He recently appeared with a Trump hat. Sort of evens out the number of Democrats and Republicans, providing for some hot political discussions.

Finally, "The Kid" in the group is a fireman and also owns a thriving business building pools. He's the most normal of all in our morning coffee klatch. Probably have enough money someday to lower the national debt. Smart, hard-working rascal. Not really a kid since he's 40 years-old, but he is much younger than all the other guys. He has a couple teenage boys, so only time will tell if he can keep his hair. They're great kids but, after all, they are teenage boys.

Yep, a diverse group, and we all live in a community called Will Rogers Equestrian Ranch. Well, except for "The Kid" who has now moved to a new, larger home nearby. And, the fellow from Ohio. Those of my generation know the story of Will Rogers. Look it up. If you can read. For your history lesson, Will Rogers was an interesting fellow from Oklahoma.

After we purchased a second home with a lawn front and back rather than the previous desert land scaping, my wife said mowing the lawn would give me exercise. Promptly reminded her that I am retired. Volunteered to purchase her an electric lawnmower if she wished, but I am not mowing grass. And, I don't. There are folks who need that work.

Our daughter Kristina gave me a small book a couple years ago with lots of questions concerning my life. No way could I stuff my life and experiences into those small pages. So, that accounts for this chronicle of that information for my children. For anyone who wants to understand how some folks "luck" into a satisfying, lifelong career, this may have been a worthwhile read. Then, maybe not. Hope that's not the case, but if it is, keep to yourself, please. Could use the money if there's an eager, well-connected publisher excited about this offering.

When beginning this wordy collection of stories about my life, the regular trips to the library each week slowed to a crawl. Recently, a couple of my favorite librarians asked why they had not seen me around. I explained about writing this little history of my life. Both said they want a copy. One said they could maybe hold a book signing for me. Imagine that. No, it's difficult for me to stretch my imagination that far. If it happens, though, they must understand that regular bathroom breaks are required. They're part of my life.

Perhaps, stranger things than a book signing for "One Eye On The World" have happened. Hey, Sean Hannity or Rush Limbaugh, can you give me a little plug? Know CNN won't since I believe everything in this is factual. Okay, okay, it is maybe based on attaining 75% my mental potential, and 75 years on earth. If that's true, content may be a tad restricted.

Many roads have been traveled and just thankful so many memories are still bouncing around in the old head. Others will likely never return, and some I would never let see daylight anyway. Everyone must have some secrets.

The World Today

As mentioned in the beginning, I have seen some of the world's wonders, and some of its disasters. Through my early years, the world moved at a slower pace. But, after World War II, the Korean Conflict and Vietnam, the United States began moving rather quickly. People previously got their news from newspapers, radio, and then television. No internet, no social media.

It was a simpler, kinder world, minus the anger we see today. Certainly for those of my generation, we remember with fondness that bygone world. Sure, people disagreed, but disagreements were often followed with a handshake. Or negotiations. Today's hate expressed by people—and politicians—could not have been imagined in earlier times. How some of the incompetent politicians even get elected remains a mystery to me. Perhaps they are the same people wanting to let 16-year-olds vote. Dumb's the word.

Current events have always played a large part in my life, and do yet today. Happenings now could easily discourage many. It seems today that many people focus primarily on events impacting their lives. That's understandable, but it is my genuine hope that people will also attempt to remember what is happening locally, statewide, nationwide and worldwide. It can affect not only them, but future generations.

Listening to social media, radio and television without a filter impacts how we view the world. Some sorry, biased newspapers also contribute. This is not shortchanging the intelligence of people, just warning that everything we read or hear is not always accurate.

Finally, coming from a career in newspapers, it saddens me to see so much bias, and failure to provide news of use to subscribers. They continue to decrease in size, page count, and news of interest. It's my hope they right the ship and once again become of importance to their readers.

It's also my hope that our politicians remember they are elected to serve those who, with their votes, placed them in office based on their promises. While we must always look to the future, we must remember lessons of the past.

Finally, it is my hope that some of this book's information will be of interest to my children. While I believe every word is factual—and at times, hopefully humorous—I would caution again of my 75 years. Oops, I just turned 76 during this writing, so please take that into consideration. Maybe I'm now working on 76% of my ability. Or, maybe it's going the other direction. Could there be another book in there somewhere? Nah, probably not, but who knows?

This is "30", a newspaper term for end of the story.

About the Author

John Shields picked cotton on a Texas farm as a child, establishing a lifetime work ethic. Starting from the bottom delivering newspapers and working in a mail room, John never thought he would become a journalist. Yet John went on to have a fifty-year career as a reporter, editor, publisher, and CEO for newspaper companies throughout the United States.